Christian Slamka

Optimal Prediction Market Design

Christian Slamka

Optimal Prediction Market Design

Market Mechanisms and Innovative Applications

Südwestdeutscher Verlag für Hochschulschriften

Impressum / Imprint
Bibliografische Information der Deutschen Nationalbibliothek: Die Deutsche Nationalbibliothek verzeichnet diese Publikation in der Deutschen Nationalbibliografie; detaillierte bibliografische Daten sind im Internet über http://dnb.d-nb.de abrufbar.
Alle in diesem Buch genannten Marken und Produktnamen unterliegen warenzeichen-, marken- oder patentrechtlichem Schutz bzw. sind Warenzeichen oder eingetragene Warenzeichen der jeweiligen Inhaber. Die Wiedergabe von Marken, Produktnamen, Gebrauchsnamen, Handelsnamen, Warenbezeichnungen u.s.w. in diesem Werk berechtigt auch ohne besondere Kennzeichnung nicht zu der Annahme, dass solche Namen im Sinne der Warenzeichen- und Markenschutzgesetzgebung als frei zu betrachten wären und daher von jedermann benutzt werden dürften.

Bibliographic information published by the Deutsche Nationalbibliothek: The Deutsche Nationalbibliothek lists this publication in the Deutsche Nationalbibliografie; detailed bibliographic data are available in the Internet at http://dnb.d-nb.de.
Any brand names and product names mentioned in this book are subject to trademark, brand or patent protection and are trademarks or registered trademarks of their respective holders. The use of brand names, product names, common names, trade names, product descriptions etc. even without a particular marking in this work is in no way to be construed to mean that such names may be regarded as unrestricted in respect of trademark and brand protection legislation and could thus be used by anyone.

Verlag / Publisher:
Südwestdeutscher Verlag für Hochschulschriften
ist ein Imprint der / is a trademark of
OmniScriptum GmbH & Co. KG
Heinrich-Böcking-Str. 6-8, 66121 Saarbrücken, Deutschland / Germany
Email: info@svh-verlag.de

Herstellung: siehe letzte Seite /
Printed at: see last page
ISBN: 978-3-8381-1147-6

Zugl. / Approved by: Frankfurt, Goethe-Universität, Dissertation, 2009

Copyright © 2009 OmniScriptum GmbH & Co. KG
Alle Rechte vorbehalten. / All rights reserved. Saarbrücken 2009

Danksagung

Die Arbeit an der Dissertation, die ich in insgesamt dreieinhalb Jahren an der Professur für Electronic Commerce an der Goethe-Universität Frankfurt anfertigte, war für mich insgesamt eine äußerst bereichernde Zeit. So konnte ich mich nicht nur in meinem hochaktuellen Thema Prognosemärkte wertvolle Erfahrungen über elektronische Märkte und E-Commerce im Allgemeinen sammeln. Auch war es sehr bereichernd, andere Sicht- und Herangehensweisen an Probleme kennenzulernen, wenn man sich von einem betriebswirtschaftlichen neben einem technischen Standpunkt nähert. Nicht zuletzt habe ich in dieser Zeit viele herausragende Menschen kennengelernt, denen ich hier danken möchte, und ohne die diese Arbeit nicht möglich gewesen wäre.

An erster Stelle möchte ich mich herzlich bei meinem Doktorvater Prof. Dr. Bernd Skiera bedanken. Er stellte stets hohe Anforderungen, was aber stets mit einem sehr großen Maß an Unterstützung und Einsatz, auch immer inhaltlich, einherging. Dank ihm konnte ich nicht nur diese Arbeit erfolgreich zu Ende bringen, sondern habe auch viele andere Aspekte, wie beispielsweise die dauernde Hinterfragung der „contribution", verinnerlicht, die mir sicherlich auch in Zukunft von großem Vorteil sein werden. Die Freiheiten, die er meinen Kollegen und mir ließ, haben das Klima am Lehrstuhl herausfordernd und zielführend, aber nie über-kompetitiv werden lassen.

Mein Dank gilt auch meinem Zweitgutachter Prof. Dr. Wolfgang König, der trotz hoher Belastung sich sehr detailliert mit der Dissertation beschäftigte. Seine vielen Mitarbeiter werde ich ebenfalls von vielen gemeinsamen Fußballspielen, sowie Trainingseinheiten und Feiern, stets in bester und lebendiger Erinnerung behalten.

Den ersten Kontakt zu Prognosemärkten bekam ich im „STOCCER"-Projekt des BmBF, auf Grund dessen ich ein drei Viertel Jahr am Institut für Informationswirtschaft und –management an der Universität Karlsruhe (TH) verbrachte. Für diese ereignisreiche Zeit mit viel abwechslungsreicher und spannender Teamarbeit, die bis zum Abschluss der Fußball-Weltmeisterschaft 2006 dauerte, möchte ich mich bei Dr. Stefan Luckner, Dr. Jan Schröder, Felix Kratzer, und natürlich Prof. Dr. Christof Weinhardt bedanken.

Dr. Arina Soukhoroukova und Prof. Dr. Martin Spann danke ich nicht nur für die gemeinsame spannende und fruchtvolle Arbeit an Projekten, sondern auch für die geteilte Begeisterung für das Thema Prognosemärkte, und insbesondere für die immer entspannte und kollegiale Zusammenarbeit. Ein weiteres besonderes Highlight der Zeit am Lehrstuhl war die gemeinsame Arbeit mit Prof. Wolfgang Jank, Ph.D., der mir dankenswerter Weise durch unser gemeinsames Projekt ermöglichte, eine ereignisreiche Zeit an der University of Maryland im Sommer 2008 zu verbringen.

Die immer positive Stimmung am Lehrstuhl und der freundschaftliche Umgang der Kollegen untereinander trugen sehr zum Spaß an der Arbeit bei. Insbesondere Frau Wernsdorf kümmerte sich immer hervorragend um das Wohlergehen und unterstützte, wo sie nur konnte. Neben den vielen Kollegen möchte ich im Besonderen meinen Bürokollegen Dr. Tanja Stepanchuk und später René Schaaf danken, mit denen es immer Grund zu angeregten Diskussionen gab, sei es über die Reinlichkeit des Büros oder die neuesten, meistens ernüchternde, Fußballergebnisse von Eintracht Frankfurt. Ebenfalls hat mir Prof. Dr. Oliver Hinz stets wertvolle Tipps gegeben und mich seiner immer freundschaftlich lockeren, aber zielgerichteten Art beeindruckt.

Einen sehr großen Anteil an der letztlich doch erfolgreichen Arbeit hatte meine liebe Freundin Jessica, die mich auch und vor allem in Zeiten unterstützte, in denen es weniger gut voran ging, wofür ich ihr immer dankbar sein werde. Ganz besonders und gewiss nicht zuletzt möchte ich meinen Eltern Dr. Paul und Doris, aber auch meinem Bruder Sebastian, danken, die mich immer unterstützten und mir Mut machten, meinen Interessen nachzugehen und eigenständig zu handeln.

Christian Slamka
Zürich, im September 2009

Inhaltsverzeichnis

Danksagung 1

I. Synopsis 9

    I.1. Einleitung 9

        I.1.1. Funktionsweise und Design von Prognosemärkten 11

        I.1.2. Kategorisierung der Anwendungen von Prognosemärkten 13

    I.2. Ziel der Dissertation 17

        I.2.1. Gesamtziel 17

        I.2.2. Überblick über die Beiträge 18

    I.3. Detaillierte Beschreibungen der Beiträge 22

        I.3.1. Prediction Market Performance and Market Liquidity: A Comparison of Automated Market Makers 22

        I.3.2. The Price of Running Liquid Prediction Markets 24

        I.3.3. Second-Generation Prediction Markets for Information Aggregation: A Comparison of Payoff Mechanisms 26

        I.3.4. An Empirical Investigation of the Forecast Accuracy of Play-Money Prediction Markets and Professional Betting Markets 28

        I.3.5. Event Studies in Real- and Play-Money Prediction Markets 30

    I.4. Fazit und Ausblick 31

II. Beiträge 39

PREDICTION MARKET PERFORMANCE AND MARKET LIQUIDITY: A COMPARISON OF AUTOMATED MARKET MAKERS 39

    1. Introduction 41

    2. Market Mechanisms 42

2.1. Overview 43
2.2. Functionality of Mechanisms 45
    2.2.1 (Logarithmic) Market Scoring Rules 45
    2.2.2 Dynamic Pari-Mutuel Market 46
    2.2.3 Dynamic Price Adjustment 48
    2.2.4 (Basic) Hollywood Stock Exchange Mechanism 50
2.3. Comparison 51

3. **Simulation Study Design** 54
    3.1. Market Microstructure 54
    3.2. Model 55
    3.3. Overview and Optimization Criterion 57
    3.4. Selection of AMM Parameters 58
    3.5. Market Environment 59

4. **Results** 60
    4.1. Forecasting accuracy 60
    4.2. Robustness Tests 63
        4.2.1 Robustness against parameter misspecification 63
        4.2.2 Robustness against noisy trading 64
    4.3. Speed of Information Incorporation 65

5. **Conclusion** 66

Appendix 71

THE PRICE OF RUNNING LIQUID PREDICTION MARKETS 79

1. **Introduction and Problem** 81
2. **Descriptions of Mechanisms** 83
    2.1. (Logarithmic) Market Scoring Rules 84
    2.2. Dynamic Pari-Mutuel Market 85
3. **Market Model** 87
    3.1. Basic Model 87

3.2.	Extension of the Model	88
4.	**Design of Simulation Study**	**89**
5.	**Results**	**91**
6.	**Conclusion and Discussion**	**94**
References		**95**

SECOND-GENERATION PREDICTION MARKETS FOR INFORMATION AGGREGATION: A COMPARISON OF PAYOFF MECHANISMS 97

1.	**Introduction**	**99**
2.	**First Generation PMs with Actual Outcome Payoff Mechanisms**	**100**
2.1.	Overview	100
2.2.	Applications	102
2.3.	Shortcomings	103
3.	**Second Generation PMs with Alternative Payoff Mechanisms**	**103**
3.1.	General Approaches	103
3.2.	Existing Studies	104
4.	**Conceptual Comparison of Payoff Mechanisms**	**105**
4.1.	Expected Accuracy of G1 and G2 Payoff Mechanisms	105
4.2.	Expected Trading Behavior in G2 PMs	106
4.2.1	Market mechanisms in PMs	106
4.2.2	Trading behavior	107
5.	**Experimental design**	**109**
6.	**Results**	**112**
6.1.	Forecast Accuracy	112
6.2.	Trading Behavior	116
6.2.1	Price difference between G1 and G2 markets	117
6.2.2	Trading volume difference between G1 and G2 markets	119
6.3.	Last Minute Trading	121

7. Conclusion 123

References 124

AN EMPIRICAL INVESTIGATION OF THE FORECAST ACCURACY OF PLAY-MONEY PREDICTION MARKETS AND PROFESSIONAL BETTING MARKETS 131

1. Introduction 133
2. Related Work 135
    2.1. Prediction Markets 135
    2.2. Fixed Odds Betting 136
3. Data Sets 137
    3.1. The FIFA World Cup 2006 137
    3.2. The STOCCER Exchange 138
    3.3. Sports Betting Odds 140
    3.4. FIFA World Ranking 141
    3.5. Random Predictor 141
4. Evaluation of the Forecast Accuracy 141
5. Summary 144

References 145

EVENT STUDIES IN REAL- AND PLAY-MONEY PREDICTION MARKETS 149

1. Introduction 151
2. Prediction Markets 153
    2.1. Idea and Theoretical Foundations of Prediction Markets 153
3. Previous Research on Continuous Reactions of Prediction Market Prices to Events and Comparisons of Play- and Real-Money Markets 154
4. Goal and Design of Empirical Study 155
    4.1. Goal of the Study 155

4.2.		Data and Requirements	155
4.3.		Prediction Market Design	157
	4.3.1	Prediction market 1 (PM1): real-money market	157
	4.3.2	Prediction market 2 (PM2): play-money market	158
4.4.		Event Study Design	158
	4.4.1	Event data collection	158
	4.4.2	Expected Return Model	159
5.		**Results of Empirical Study**	**160**
5.1.		Evaluation Criteria	160
5.2.		Evaluation Results	161
	5.2.1	Magnitude of stock price reactions and stability of returns	161
	5.2.2	Speed of information incorporation	164
	5.2.3	Change of predictive accuracy	165
	5.2.4	Liquidity	167
6.		**General Discussion**	**168**
References			**169**
Appendix: Standard Procedure of Event Studies			**172**

I. Synopsis

I.1. Einleitung

Die Vorhersage von unsicheren zukünftigen Ereignissen, auf der Entscheidungen in Unternehmen aufbauen, ist eine grundlegende Herausforderung in der Unternehmensplanung. Inakkurate oder zu spät abgegebene Vorhersagen, beispielsweise von Verkaufszahlen von Produkten, können zu substantiellen Kosten für Unternehmen führen (Spann und Skiera, 2003). Durch immer kürzer werdende Produktzyklen und die zunehmende Globalisierung von Märkten wird es zudem für Unternehmen immer komplexer und damit schwieriger, zukünftige Entwicklungen, Trends, Potenziale, Herausforderungen oder auch Risiken vorherzusehen (Luckner, 2008). Daraus ergibt sich, dass sich beispielsweise traditionelle Vorhersagemethoden, die auf der Analyse von Vergangenheitsdaten beruhen, auf Grund des sich schnell ändernden Umfelds nicht angewendet werden können. Stattdessen wird heutzutage zunehmend versucht, auf Informationen über den Ausgang zukünftiger Ereignisse zurückzugreifen, die auf viele Personen asymmetrisch verteilt sind, beispielsweise bei Neuproduktentwicklungen. Es gibt hier also nicht mehr nur eine oder wenige Quellen von Informationen, wie z.B. wenige Experten mit „allumfassendem" Wissen, sondern viele von einander unabhängige Personen, die verschiedene relevante Informationen besitzen.

Bei Nutzung dieser Informationen entstehen aber auf der anderen Seite neue Herausforderungen, vor allem bezüglich a) der Aufdeckung relevanter Informationen unter einer großen Menge von Informationen, b) deren Wahrheitsgehalt und c) deren Aggregationsform, d.h. wie viele Einzelmeinungen zu einer Gesamtmeinung zusammengeführt werden können. Prognosemärkte haben hier in den letzten Jahren verstärkt an Bedeutung gewonnen, da sie genau diese drei zentralen Herausforderungen adressieren (Wolfers und Zitzewitz, 2004). In Prognosemärkten werden Ereignisse, deren Ausgänge vorherzusagen sind, als virtuelle Aktien abgebildet, woraufhin diese über das Internet mit entweder Spiel- oder Echtgeld gehandelt werden können. Durch Darstellung der Ereignisse als Aktien in Märkten wird Teilnehmern ein starker Anreiz geboten, stets ihre aktuellen, wahrheitsgemäßen Informationen in die Aktienpreise einfließen zu lassen.

Prognosemärkten sind somit in der Lage, Ereignisse meist besser zu prognostizieren als alternative Instrumente, wie z.B. Umfragen oder offizielle Unternehmensvorhersagen, was in verschiedenen Studien gezeigt wurde (z.B. Berg et al., 2008, Chen und Plott, 2002, Spann et al., 2009, Spann und Skiera, 2009, Wolfers und Zitzewitz, 2004). Daneben weisen Prognosemärkte weitere Vorteile gegenüber alternativen Instrumenten auf, wie z.b. geringere Kosten (Dahan et al., 2009) oder Skalierbarkeit in Bezug auf beispielsweise die Anzahl der Teilnehmer oder der Aktien (Soukhoroukova und Spann, 2006). Dabei sind die Anwendungsgebiete, in denen Prognosemärkte eingesetzt werden, äußerst vielfältig (Soukhoroukova und Spann, 2006): In der Politik werden sie als Wahlbörsen eingesetzt (Berg et al., 2003, Berg et al., 2008, Forsythe et al., 1992), in der Wirtschaft z.B. zur Prognose von Verkaufszahlen (Chen und Plott, 2002, Ortner, 1998) oder in Gebieten wie der Medizin zur Prognose der Verbreitung von Vogelgrippeviren (Holden, 2007).

In den vorgenannten Beispielen der Anwendung von Prognosemärkten muss das vorherzusagende Ereignis noch in einem kurz- oder mittelfristigen Zeitraum eintreten, um den Teilnehmern einen Anreiz zu geben, ihre Informationen wahrheitsgemäß offenzulegen (Wolfers und Zitzewitz, 2004, Spann und Skiera, 2003). Bei diesen Prognosemärkten der „ersten Generation" ist also die Bandbreite der Anwendungen noch stark beschränkt. Bei Prognosemärkten der „zweiten Generation" aber, die in den letzten Jahren entwickelt wurden (z.B. Dahan et al., 2009, LaComb et al., 2007, Soukhoroukova et al., 2008), muss kein „wahres", d.h. extern validierbares, Ereignis mehr vorhanden sein. Ereignisse können also erst nach längerer Zeit (etwa nach mehreren Jahren) eintreten, wie bei langfristigen Prognosen, oder auch nie, wie bei der Wahl zwischen Alternativen auf Basis der Vorhersage ihrer wahrscheinlichen Potenziale. Zusätzlich ist es hier möglich, eigene Aktien durch Teilnehmer als Ideen vorschlagen und bewerten zu lassen (LaComb et al., 2007, Soukhoroukova et al., 2008).

Neben dem Interesse der Forschung am Thema Prognosemärkte hat sich auch in der Praxis ein neuer Industriezweig gebildet, dessen acht führende Unternehmen sich in der „Prediction Market Industry Association" (www.pmindustry.org) als Interessensvertretung zusammengeschlossen haben und gemeinsam die Verbreitung von Prognosemärkten vorantreiben. Hierbei kann auch beobachtet werden, dass Anbieter von Prognosemärkten ihr Dienstleistungsportfolio von reinen Märkten der „ersten Generation" zu Märkten der „zweiten Generation" stark ausgeweitet haben. Beispiele hierfür sind z.B. NewsFutures (www.newsfutures.com, „Idea Pageant"), einer der führenden Anbieter von Prognosemarkt-

Diensten, Nosco (www.nosco.com, „Idea Exchange") oder auch XPress (www.xpree.com, „Open Innovation Markets").

I.1.1. Funktionsweise und Design von Prognosemärkten

Auf einem Prognosemarkt wird ein unsicheres, zukünftiges Ereignis mittels einer virtuellen Aktie handelbar gemacht (z.B. der prozentuale Stimmanteil einer Partei bei einer Wahl, die Wahrscheinlichkeit der Einhaltung eines Projektzeitplans oder die Absatzzahlen eines Produktes). Bei Prognosemärkten der „ersten Generation" richtet sich der Endwert der Aktien, d.h. die Auszahlung, dabei nach der tatsächlichen Ausprägung des vorherzusagenden Ereignisses. Eine Aktie kann deshalb bei Marktschluss bspw. einen Euro pro erreichtem Prozentpunkt bei einer Wahl, einen Euro bei Einhaltung eines internen Projektzeitplans oder einen Euro pro verkauften tausend Einheiten eines Produktes wert sein (Spann und Skiera, 2003, Wolfers und Zitzewitz, 2004).

Unter der Annahme der Rationalität verkaufen Teilnehmer Aktien, die sie nach ihrem privaten Informationsstand als zu hoch bewertet einschätzen, d.h. ihren endgültigen Preis niedriger einschätzen. Dagegen kaufen Teilnehmer Aktien, falls sie deren zukünftigen Preis höher einschätzen (Glosten und Milgrom, 1985). Der aktuelle Preis einer Aktie entspricht also den aggregierten Erwartungen der Teilnehmer (Spann und Skiera, 2003). Hierbei ist der Marktmechanismus das effizienteste Instrument, um asymmetrische, d.h. verschiedene, auf Teilnehmer verteilte Informationen zu aggregieren (Hayek, 1945). Falls nun alle Informationen im aktuellen Preis einer Aktie reflektiert sind, so wird er als *effizient* bezeichnet (Fama, 1970, Fama, 1991). In diesem Fall können anhand des Preises der Aktie also Rückschlüsse auf die tatsächliche Ausprägung des vorherzusagenden Ereignisses getroffen werden.

Mangels externer Validierbarkeit wird bei Prognosemärkten der „zweiten Generation" die Ausprägung eines Ereignisses durch Proxy-Werte angenähert. Hier können marktinterne Handelsdaten (z.B. Dahan et al., 2009) oder auch externe Experten (Graefe und Weinhardt, 2008, Soukhoroukova et al., 2008) zur Annäherung herangezogen werden. Es ist bis heute jedoch nicht untersucht, wie effizient die Preise und wie gut damit die Prognosen dieser neuen Form der Prognosemärkte tatsächlich sind.

Um aber das Zustandekommen eines effizienten Preises zu gewährleisten, muss bei Prognosemärkten der „ersten" wie auch der „zweiten Generation" das Marktdesign optimal gewählt werden. Dies impliziert, dass die Gestaltung der Märkte systematisch zu erfolgen hat (Weinhardt et al., 2003). Spann und Skiera (2003) haben hierzu drei grundlegende Schritte zum Design von Prognosemärkten herausgearbeitet (siehe auch Abbildung 1), die im Folgenden mit den bisherigen Forschungsergebnissen dargestellt sind:

- Die *Auswahl des Prognoseziels* beinhaltet Designparameter wie die Auswahl des vorherzusagenden Ereignisses, die Auszahlungsfunktion oder den Teilnehmerkreis. Bis heute gibt es relativ wenige Forschungsarbeiten aus diesem Bereich. Es existieren allgemeine Diskussionen über die Auswahl des Prognoseziels (Graefe, 2008, Spann und Skiera, 2003, Wolfers und Zitzewitz, 2004). Christiansen (2007) zeigt empirisch in Bezug auf den Teilnehmerkreis, dass auch eine geringe Anzahl an Teilnehmern von einem Dutzend Personen gute Prognoseergebnisse liefern kann. Weiterhin zeigen Gruca et al. (2003), allerdings mit einer sehr kleinen Anzahl an Beobachtungen, dass offene Märkte, bei denen jeder Teilnehmer ohne Vorauswahl handeln kann, bessere Prognosen liefern als solche mit geschlossenem, d.h. fest vordefiniertem, Teilnehmerkreis.

- Durch die *Gestaltung der Anreizstruktur* werden Teilnehmer von Prognosemärkten dazu angeregt, überhaupt zu handeln und ihre persönlichen Einschätzungen über den Ausgang eines Ereignisses preiszugeben. Servan-Schreiber et al. (2004) haben hierbei festgestellt, dass Spielgeld-Prognosemärkte ähnlich gut prognostizieren wie Echtgeld-Prognosemärkte. Diese Ergebnisse werden allerdings von Rosenbloom und Notz (2006) dahingehend relativiert, dass der Unterschied abhängig vom Anwendungsgebiet ist. Luckner und Weinhardt (2007) untersuchen verschiedene Entlohnungsmechanismen von Teilnehmern und stellen heraus, dass solche mit einer implementierten Rangfolge, bei denen die Teilnehmer relativ zu einander entlohnt werden, die besten Ergebnisse liefern. Darüber hinaus zeigt Christiansen (2007), dass nicht unbedingt extrinsische Anreize, z.B. in Form von Preisen, vorhanden sein müssen, damit gute Prognoseergebnisse erzielt werden können.

- Schließlich gilt es, das *Handelsdesign* festzulegen, insbesondere in Bezug auf Designparameter wie Marktmechanismen, Ordertypen oder Handelsgebühren. In der Literatur werden einige Vorschläge für verschiedene neuartige Marktmechanismen, so genannte

„Automatisierte Market Maker", unterbreitet (z.B. Hanson, 2007, Pennock, 2004), die das in Prognosemärkten allgegenwärtige Problem der Illiquidität durch kontinuierlich möglichen Handel zu adressieren versuchen. Jedoch gibt es bis dato keine Evaluationen verschiedener Marktmechanismen. Einzig Geyer-Schulz et al. (2007) vergleichen zwei auch in Finanzmärkten übliche Marktmechanismen (doppelte kontinuierliche Auktion und Call-Auktion) bezüglich ihrer Prognosegüte, stellen aber keine nennenswerten Unterschiede fest. Oliven und Rietz (2004) zeigen, dass ein Prognosemarkt trotz der Anwesenheit von uninformierten, irrationalen Händlern auf Grund von informierten Händlern, die Preise setzen, effizient sein kann.

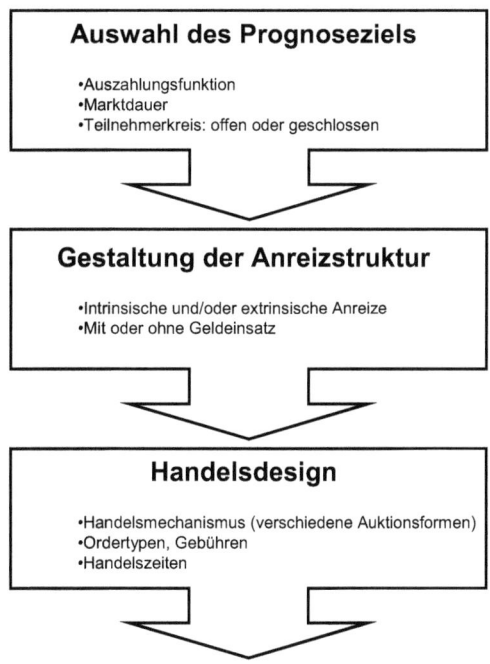

Abbildung 1: Design von Prognosemärkten (aus Spann und Skiera, 2003, Spann et al., 2006)

I.1.2. Kategorisierung der Anwendungen von Prognosemärkten

Durch die steigende Anzahl an Anwendungen von Prognosemärkten werden diese für eine bessere Zuordnung anhand zweier Kriterien klassifiziert (Abbildung 2), um die wichtigsten Unterschiede herauszustellen. Hierbei wird nicht auf einzelne Anwendungsgebiete eingegangen (dazu siehe z.B. Spann und Skiera, 2004), sondern auf den generellen, strukturellen Aufbau der Anwendung.

Das erste Kriterium unterscheidet Prognosemärkte dahingehend, ob es sich um Prognosemärkte der „ersten" oder „zweiten Generation" handelt, d.h. ob die zu untersuchenden Ereignisse kurz- bzw. mittelfristig eintreten und damit validierbar sind.

Das zweite Kriterium bezieht sich auf die Nutzung der vielfältigen Daten, die in den Märkten durch Handeln der Teilnehmer über den gesamten Handelszeitraum hinweg entstehen. Während einerseits nur der letzte gehandelte Preis einer Aktie als einziges Ergebnis des Marktes verwendet werden kann, ist es andererseits auch möglich, darüber hinaus gehende Handelsdaten zu verwerten. Auf Aktienebene kann beispielsweise der dynamische Handelsverlauf einer Aktie betrachtet werden, oder auf Teilnehmerebene einzelne Handelsaktionen oder die Gesamtleistung.

Durch diese Klassifikation entsteht eine 2-x-2-Matrix, die mit Beispielen in Abbildung 2 dargestellt ist.

		Vorherzusagendes Ereignis tritt kurz- oder mittelfristig ein	
		Ja (Prognosemärkte der „ersten Generation")	Nein (Prognosemärkte der „zweiten Generation")
Daten-nutzung	Letzter Preis (Punkt-prognose)	• *Kurz- und mittelfristige Punktprognosen* (z.B. Berg et al., 2008; Spann und Skiera, 2003)	• *Konzepttests* (Chan et al., 2002; Dahan et al., 2009; Soukhoroukova und Spann, 2005) • *Ideengenerierung* (LaComb et al., 2007; Soukhoroukova et al., 2008)
	Weitergehende Handelsdaten	• *Ereignisstudien* (z.B. Elberse, 2007) • *Frühe Prognosen* (Jank und Foutz, 2009) • *Expertenidentifikation* (Spann et al., 2009)	• *noch keine* (Ereignisstudien bei Konzepttests vorgeschlagen in Dahan et al. (2009))

Abbildung 2: Kategorisierung der Anwendungen von Prognosemärkten bezüglich Eintritt des Ereignisses und Datennutzung

Bei der Mehrzahl der Anwendungen von Prognosemärkten (linker oberer Quadrant) werden fast ausschließlich Fälle betrachtet, in denen das vorherzusagende Ereignis in einem kurz- bzw. mittelfristigen Zeitraum eintritt (z.B. Berg et al., 2008, Spann und Skiera, 2003). Darüber hinaus wird ein einziger Wert, meist der letzte Handelspreis der Aktie, als Prognose für das eintretende Ereignis herangezogen, d.h. eine Punktprognose abgegeben.

Während bei Prognosemärkten der „ersten Generation" noch eine große Beschränkung bezüglich der vorherzusagenden Ereignisse besteht, ist dies bei Prognosemärkten der „zweiten Generation", die auch Punktprognosen erheben können, nicht mehr der Fall (rechter oberer Quadrant). In der Anwendung bei nicht eintretenden Ereignissen haben Konzepttests (Chan et al., 2002, Dahan et al., 2009, Soukhoroukova und Spann, 2005) gezeigt, dass die Evaluation von Produktkonzepten als Wahl aus Alternativen mit Prognosemärkten durchführbar ist. Dadurch können Vorteile bezüglich der Skalierbarkeit (beispielsweise im Hinblick auf die Anzahl der Teilnehmer oder der Aktien), der Kosten der Prognose oder der Abschwächung von einzelnen verzerrten Meinungen der Teilnehmer realisiert werden. Erweitert um die Option, Ideen bzw. Konzepte selbst vorzuschlagen, finden auch Ideenmärkte (LaComb et al., 2007, Soukhoroukova et al., 2008) in letzter Zeit verstärkte Anwendung. Trotz dieser Aufmerksamkeit in Theorie und Praxis ist es durch die fehlende Verfügbarkeit eines externen, objektiven Benchmarks bei nicht eintretenden Ereignissen bislang nicht gelungen, die Prognosequalität der Prognosemärkte der „zweiten Generation" zu bestimmen.

Weitere Anwendungen basieren auf Prognosemärkten der „ersten Generation", wobei allerdings nicht nur der letzte Preis als Datengrundlage herangezogen wird (linker unterer Quadrant in Abbildung 2), sondern auch weitergehende Handelsdaten genutzt werden. Insbesondere sind hier die Preisdynamiken von Interesse, d.h. die Entwicklung der Aktienpreise über die Zeit. Elberse (2007) untersucht in einer Ereignisstudie den Einfluss von Stars auf den Erfolg von Filmen durch eine Analyse der Preisreaktionen von virtuellen Aktien einer Filmbörse auf die Ankündigung der Teilnahme von Stars in Filmen. Die Analyse der Entwicklung von Aktienpreisen über die Zeit mittels „funktionaler Datenanalyse" (Ramsay und Silverman, 2005) kann auch dabei helfen, frühe, d.h. nicht kurz vor dem Eintritt des Ereignisses stehende, Prognosen zu verbessern (Foutz und Jank, 2008). Um Experten zu identifizieren (z.B. „Lead User"), greifen Spann et al. (2009) auf Portfoliodaten der individuellen Teilnehmer zurück und zeigen, dass ein substantieller Anteil von „Lead Usern" unter den Teilnehmern mit hohem Portfoliowert existiert.

Ein bisher offenes Forschungsfeld bleibt hier noch die Anwendung von Prognosemärkten der „zweiten Generation" über reine Punktprognosen hinaus (rechter unterer Quadrant in Abbildung 2). Zwar haben Dahan et al. (2009) mit Ereignisstudien bei Produktkonzepttests erste Anwendungen vorgeschlagen, jedoch sollten hierbei zunächst die grundlegenden Designfragen der Anwendungen im oberen rechten und unteren linken Quadranten in Abbildung 2 (insb. Ereignisstudien) geklärt sein.

Zusammenfassend ist zu sagen, dass nach dem aktuellen Stand der Forschung und Praxis bereits einige, in den letzten Jahren auch sehr innovative, Anwendungen von Prognosemärkten gefunden werden konnten. Allerdings ist bislang unklar, unter welchen Vorraussetzungen und insbesondere mit welcher Ausgestaltung möglicher Designparameter Prognosemärkte optimal zum Einsatz kommen können. Dabei ist die Wahl des Designs für Betreiber von Prognosemärkten essentiell, um effiziente Aktienpreise in den Märkten realisieren zu können. Denn effiziente Preise sind in Prognosemärkten die Grundvoraussetzung für die Erreichung des eigentlichen Ziels der Anwendung, beispielsweise eine hohe Prognosegüte oder eine schnelle Reaktion der Preise auf neue Informationen im Markt.

I.2. Ziel der Dissertation

I.2.1. Gesamtziel

Das Ziel der Dissertation besteht darin, grundlegende Designparameter von Prognosemärkten der „ersten" und „zweiten Generation" zu untersuchen und daraus Gestaltungsempfehlungen für den optimalen Einsatz abzuleiten. Diesbezüglich können zwei Themenkomplexe unterschieden werden (siehe auch Abbildung 3), *Marktmechanismen* und *Anwendungen*.

Im ersten Komplex werden verschiedene *Marktmechanismen* sowohl konzeptionell als auch experimentell evaluiert, welche die Grundlage für einen effizienten Preisfindungsprozess in einem Prognosemarkt bilden (siehe „Handelsdesign" in Abschnitt I.1.1). Dabei ist diese Forschung unabhängig von den eigentlichen Anwendungen, die in Abschnitt I.1.2 beschrieben werden; sie ist vielmehr Grundvoraussetzung für effiziente Preise. Hier werden also die Grundlagen für den erfolgreichen Einsatz von Prognosemärkten gelegt, auf denen dann beliebige Anwendungen aufbauen können. Konkret spielen bei Prognosemärkten vor allem die automatisierten Market Maker eine große Rolle, die fortlaufend An- und Verkaufspreise bereitstellen und dadurch Aktien jederzeit handelbar machen. Es können sich aber, je nach Parametrisierung, große Abweichungen in der Qualität der Prognose ergeben (Christiansen, 2007). Trotz wachsender Verbreitung und auch steigendem Einsatz in der Praxis wurde bislang jedoch weder ein Vergleich zwischen Market Makern durchgeführt, noch wurden konkrete Handlungsempfehlungen zu deren Parametrisierung oder zum Einsatz in verschiedenen Szenarien gegeben. Dem Themenkomplex Marktmechanismen lassen sich die Beiträge #1 und #2 der Dissertation zuordnen.

Der zweite Themenkomplex *Anwendungen* beschäftigt sich mit der optimalen Ausgestaltung der Designparametern von Anwendungen, die in Abschnitt I.1.2 beschrieben wurden. Hierbei ist jeder der drei Beiträge der Dissertation in die Kategorisierung der Anwendungen (Abbildung 2) eingeordnet. Für jeden der drei Quadranten in Abbildung 2, bei denen bereits Anwendungen bestehen (linker oberer, rechter oberer, linker unterer), werden jeweils die Anwendbarkeit sowie das optimale Design der Anwendungen analysiert und bestimmt. Den verschiedenen Schritten des systematischen Designs eines Prognosemarktes (Abschnitt I.1.1) können die drei verbleibenden Beiträge der Dissertation wie folgt zugeordnet werden: „Auswahl des Prognoseziels" (Beitrag #3) und „Gestaltung der Anreizstruktur" (Beiträge #4 und #5).

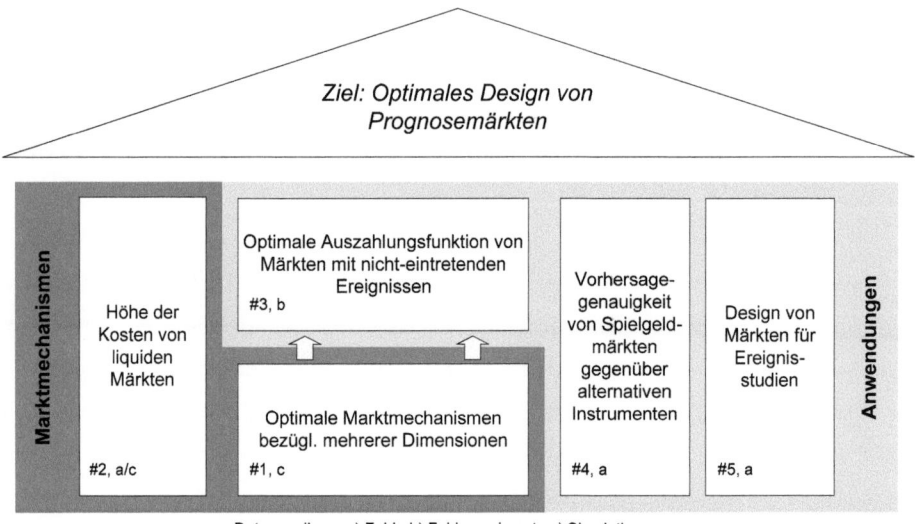

Abbildung 3: Aufbau und Ziel der Dissertation

I.2.2. Überblick über die Beiträge

Im Folgenden wird ein kurzer Überblick über die einzelnen Beiträge der Dissertation gegeben. Tabelle 1 veranschaulicht die genauen Ziele sowie die Daten und Methoden der einzelnen Beiträge.

In Beitrag #1 werden existierende Market Maker detailliert beschrieben und deren Funktionsweisen und Eigenschaften konzeptionell verglichen. Hierbei spielen einerseits die mögliche Anwendungsbreite der Mechanismen sowie deren grundsätzliche Eigenschaften eine große Rolle, anderseits aber auch die leichte Anwendbarkeit für Teilnehmer der Märkte. Mit Hilfe eines speziell für diese Market Maker entwickelten mikroökonomischen Modells werden durch Simulationen Analysen in mehreren Zieldimensionen durchgeführt und für jede Zieldimension der geeignete Mechanismus bestimmt. Auf Basis der Identifikation des geeigneten Mechanismus wird der Market Maker für die Anwendung in Beitrag #3 ausgewählt.

Beitrag #2 untersucht als Erweiterung von Beitrag #1, mit wie viel Geld Prognosemärkte mit Market Makern bezuschusst werden müssen, damit optimale Prognoseergebnisse entstehen können. Durch Hinzunehmen von Daten aus einem realen Echtgeld-Prognosemarkt in die Simulation ist es möglich, absolute Zahlen zur Bezuschussung sowie Unterschiede zwischen den einzelnen Market Makern zu bestimmen.

Beitrag #3 ist dem oberen rechten Quadranten aus Abbildung 2 zuzuordnen und bestimmt erstmals die Prognosegüte verschiedener alternativer Auszahlungsmechanismen der Aktien von Prognosemärkten der „zweiten Generation". Ziel ist es, den Auszahlungsmechanismus mit der höchsten Prognosegüte zu identifizieren. Hierzu wird ein Prognosemarkt der „ersten Generation" als Benchmark genutzt. Zusätzlich wird das Handelsverhalten, das zuvor konzeptionell untersucht wird, in den Märkten mit den verschiedenen Auszahlungsmechanismen analysiert. Die Daten stammen hierbei aus einem eigens durchgeführten Feldexperiment über drei Themenkomplexe, bei dem der in Beitrag #1 identifizierte optimale Marktmechanismus eingesetzt wird.

Beitrag #4 untersucht anhand einer kurz-/mittelfristigen Prognose (linker oberer Quadrant), ob Spielgeldmärkte ähnlich gut prognostizieren können wie Instrumente mit realen, sehr hohen ökonomischen Anreizen. Bei Spielgeldmärkten können Teilnehmer im Gegensatz zu alternativen Instrumenten keine finanziellen Verluste erleiden. Darüber hinaus wird die Prognosegüte mit Daten aus der Vergangenheit sowie einer Zufallsziehung verglichen. Die Daten des Prognosemarktes stammen aus einer eigens durchgeführten Feldstudie zur Fußball-Weltmeisterschaft 2006 mit insgesamt über 1800 Teilnehmern und über 1600 Transaktionen durchschnittlich pro Tag. Hierbei werden zwei Markttypen untersucht, die einerseits jedes Spiel und andererseits das gesamte Turnier vorhersagen.

Mit Prognosemärkten der „ersten Generation" und einer Analyse der Preisänderungen im Markt als Reaktion auf Ereignisse untersucht Beitrag #5, der im linken unteren

Quadranten in Abbildung 2 angesiedelt ist, ob Prognosemärkte überhaupt für Ereignisstudien geeignet sind und wie schnell sie auf Ereignisse reagieren. Hierbei wird vor allem untersucht, ob und welche Unterschiede zwischen Echtgeld- und Spielgeldmärkten in verschiedenen Dimensionen bestehen. Es werden hier zwei große Felddatensätze von professionellen Wettanbietern verglichen, die jeweils mehrere Tausend Händler und mehrere Zehntausend Transaktionen beinhalten. Zusätzlich kommen aufgezeichnete Informationen über Ereignisse zum Einsatz.

Beitrag/Autoren	Titel	Ziele	Methoden/Daten
#1 Slamka, Skiera, Spann	*Prediction Market Performance and Market Liquidity: A Comparison of Automated Market Makers*	• Einheitliche Beschreibung und konzeptioneller Vergleich existierender Market-Maker-Marktmechanismen • Experimentelle Evaluation der Market Maker hinsichtlich mehrerer Zieldimensionen	• Konzeptioneller Vergleich • Mikroökonomisches Modell • Simulation
#2 Slamka	*The Price of Running Liquid Prediction Markets*	• Bestimmung der maximalen und erwarteten monetären Zuschüsse, die ein Market Maker für den Handel benötigt • Bestimmung der Abhängigkeit der Zuschüsse von der Marktdauer	• Theoretische Analyse • Simulation unter Einbeziehung von Felddaten
#3 Slamka, Jank, Skiera	*Second-Generation Prediction Markets for Information Aggregation: A Comparison of Payoff Mechanisms*	• Untersuchung der Prognosegüte von Prognosemärkten mit alternativen Auszahlungsmechanismen • Konzeptionelle und empirische Analyse der Handelsstrategien von Händlern in Märkten mit alternativen Auszahlungsmechanismen	• Konzeptioneller Vergleich • Analyse von Daten aus Feldexperiment

#4 Slamka, Luckner, Seemann, Schröder	*An Empirical Investigation of the Forecast Accuracy of Play-Money Prediction Markets and Professional Betting Markets*	• Vergleich der Prognosegüte von Spielgeld-Prognosemärkten gegenüber
		  • professionellen Wettanbietern
		  • Vergangenheitsdaten
		  • Zufallsziehung
			• Analyse von Daten aus Feldstudie

#5 Slamka, Soukhoroukova, Spann	*Event Studies in Real- and Play-Money Prediction Markets*	• Untersuchung der Eignung und Unterschiede von Spiel- und Echtgeldmärkten für die Ereignisanalyse • Aufzeigung der möglichen Voraussetzungen für Ereignisanalyse in Prognosemärkten mit Spiel-/Echtgeld	• Analyse von zwei Felddatensätzen auf Transaktionsbasis • Zusammenführung mit Daten aus aufgezeichneten Ereignissen

Tabelle 1: Aufstellung der Beiträge mit einzelnen Zielen und Methoden/Daten

I.3. Detaillierte Beschreibungen der Beiträge

I.3.1. Prediction Market Performance and Market Liquidity: A Comparison of Automated Market Makers

In den Anfängen von Prognosemärkten wurde als Marktmechanismus meist die kontinuierliche doppelte Auktion gewählt, wie z.B. bei den Iowa Electronic Markets (Forsythe et al., 1992, Forsythe et al., 1999). Hier kann jeder Teilnehmer Kauf- bzw. Verkaufsgebote für eine im Grunde beliebige Anzahl an Aktien abgeben. Wenn durch ein Kaufgebot ein für ein Verkaufsgebot ausreichend hoher Preis entsteht, wird die Transaktion durchgeführt. Auf Grund der sehr niedrigen Liquidität in Prognosemärkten setzen Betreiber von Prognosemärkten aber fast ausschließlich sogenannte *automatisierte Market Maker* ein, deren Algorithmen jederzeit Kauf- und Verkaufskurse stellen und somit „unendliche" Liquidität garantieren. Gerade in Märkten mit wenigen Teilnehmern und/oder einer großen Anzahl von Aktien sind Market Maker essentiell für kontinuierliche Handelsmöglichkeiten. Trotz der Wichtigkeit des Marktmechanismus für die Prognosegüte (Christiansen, 2007, Spann und Skiera, 2003) wurden in der Literatur bisher keine Vergleiche zwischen verschiedenen Market Makern unternommen. Es ist bis heute also nicht klar, welcher Market Maker in welchen Situationen die besten Prognoseergebnisse liefert. Darüber hinaus fehlt es sogar teilweise an vollständigen Beschreibungen der Market Maker.

Ziel des Beitrags #1 ist es daher, zunächst die vier bestehenden Market Maker in einem einheitlichen Bezugsrahmen zu beschreiben, sie auf einer konzeptionellen Ebene zu vergleichen und dann mittels einer Simulation experimentell gegenüberzustellen.

Grundsätzlich können die Market Maker dahingehend klassifiziert werden, ob ihnen eine kontinuierliche Preisfunktion zu Grunde liegt. Die beiden Market Maker *Logarithmic Market Scoring Rules* (*LMSR*, Hanson, 2003, Hanson, 2007) und *Dynamic Pari-Mutuel Market* (*DPM*, Pennock, 2004) basieren auf einer solchen kontinuierlichen Preisfunktion, anhand derer An- und Verkaufspreise bestimmt werden. Ferner sind diese Market Maker arbitragefrei, d.h. durch geschicktes An- und Verkaufen kann kein Gewinn erzielt werden.

Bei den anderen beiden Market Makern, dem *Dynamic Price Adjustment* (*DPA*, Soukhoroukova et al., 2008, Van Bruggen et al., 2008) und dem *Hollywood Stock Exchange Mechanism* (*HSX*, Keiser und Burns, 1999, Keiser und Burns, 2003, Keiser und Burns, 2006) existiert keine kontinuierliche Preisfunktion. Hier werden die Aktienpreise erst nach bzw. vor der Orderausführung bestimmt und sind konstant.

Aus dem konzeptionellen Vergleich lässt sich hauptsächlich schließen, dass der DPM bezüglich der Anwendbarkeit von Aktientypen sowie Bedienbarkeit einige Nachteile gegenüber den anderen Market Makern aufweist. Der HSX besitzt den entscheidenden Nachteil, dass erst über einen gewissen Zeitraum Aktienorders gesammelt werden, so dass der Handelspreis bei der Orderabgabe noch nicht feststeht.

Da die Parametrisierung der Mechanismen und die Unabhängigkeit von den Teilnehmern einen entscheidenden Einfluss auf das Marktergebnis haben, wird eine Simulation zur Evaluation angewandt. Abweichungen der Marktergebnisse können so exakt auf den jeweiligen Mechanismus und dessen Parametrisierung zurückgeführt werden. Um die Simulation durchzuführen, wird zunächst ein mikroökonomisches Modell entworfen, welches für risikoneutrale, nutzenmaximierende Teilnehmer bestimmt, welche Aktie und welche Anzahl sie zu kaufen bzw. zu verkaufen haben. Dies wird für jeden Market Maker im Marktmodell gesondert bestimmt, während die Umweltparameter, d.h. beispielsweise Wertschätzungen von Aktien, davon unberührt bleiben.

In der Simulation werden die Market Maker anhand insgesamt vier verschiedener Dimensionen evaluiert. In der ersten Dimension, der durchschnittlichen Prognosegüte mit optimal eingestellten Parametern, zeigt sich, dass der DPM die besten Ergebnisse erbringt, allerdings nahe an denen des LMSR. Der DPA erzeugt einen mehr als doppelt so hohen Fehler wie der DPM, während der Fehler beim HSX fast drei Mal so hoch ist.

Hinsichtlich der zweiten Dimension, der Robustheit der Ergebnisse gegenüber einer Parameter-Misspezifikation, schneiden die Market Maker mit kontinuierlicher Preisfunktion wieder besser ab. Weitaus schlechter ist hier das Ergebnis des HSX, allerdings weniger schlecht als das des DPA, der bei einem zu niedrigen Parameterwert von 75% einen höheren Fehler von mehreren einhundert Prozent liefert.

Ein Nachteil von LMSR und DPM wird bei der Analyse der Robustheit gegen nicht exakt informierte Teilnehmer, die nicht den exakten wahren Wert der Aktie kennen, deutlich (dritte Dimension). Hier steigt der Fehler signifikant sowohl mit der Anzahl der nicht exakt informierten Teilnehmer als auch mit der Intensität der Abweichung vom wahren Wert. Weil der HSX aber mit einer Orderakkumulierung arbeitet, haben diese Händler keinen Einfluss auf den Fehler. Der DPA schneidet hierbei kaum besser als LMSR und DPM ab.

Als letzte Dimension wird die Geschwindigkeit, in der die Market Maker neue Informationen komplett eingepreist haben, betrachtet. Wie auch bei der Prognosegüte sind hier DPM und LMSR vergleichbar gut, DPA deutlich schlechter und HSX abgeschlagen.

Zusammenfassend zeigt Beitrag #1, dass bezüglich einer Gesamtbewertung der LMSR deutlich besser als die anderen Mechanismen abschneidet. Neben positiv zu bewertenden allgemeinen Eigenschaften, wie die Unterstützung mehrerer Aktiendesigns, zeigt der LMSR ebenfalls gute Ergebnisse in den durchgeführten Simulationen. Der DPM liefert zwar sehr gute Ergebnisse in den Simulationen, hat aber Schwächen in der Anwendbarkeit. Der HSX kann insbesondere dann von Interesse sein, wenn sich viele nicht exakt informierte Händler im Market befinden, da einzelne Händler weniger das Gesamtergebnis beeinflussen. Es ist hingegen schwierig, positive Punkte außer einem einheitlichen An- und Verkaufspreis für den DPA zu finden.

Dieser Beitrag gibt somit zum ersten Mal in der Literatur einen kompletten Überblick über bestehende Market Maker, vergleicht diese konzeptionell und bestimmt anhand verschiedener Dimensionen den jeweils optimalen Marktmechanismus. Damit kann Praktikern, d.h. Betreibern von Prognosemärkten, eine fundierte Entscheidungshilfe zur Auswahl des für sie optimalen Mechanismus, aber auch bei der Wahl der Parameter gegeben werden, um so möglichst effiziente Preise zu erreichen.

I.3.2. The Price of Running Liquid Prediction Markets

Bislang werden Market Maker sowohl in der Praxis als auch in der Forschung ausschließlich in Spielgeld-Prognosemärkten eingesetzt. Dies liegt vor allem an der Tatsache, dass Market Maker als Marktmechanismus subventioniert werden müssen. Durch den Einsatz von Market Makern entstehen Marktbetreibern etwaige Kosten durch z.B. billige Verkaufspreise von Aktien an Teilnehmer, die aber nach der Festlegung des Endwertes einen höheren Wert haben können. Aus diesem Grund werden kontinuierliche doppelte Auktionen, bei welchen Transaktionen im Wesentlichen nur zwischen Teilnehmern stattfinden, in Echtgeld-Prognosemärkten wie Betfair (www.betfair.com) eingesetzt. Hingegen können Market Maker Vorteile in Echtgeld-Prognosemärkten bieten, falls sie vergleichsweise illiquide sind. Echtgeld-Prognosemärkte können außerdem dahingehend vorteilhaft sein, als dass sie keine materiellen Preise als Anreiz benötigen, für deren Kauf und Abwicklung wiederum Kosten entstehen würden. Die Frage dieses Beitrages ist also, wie viel Geld nötig ist, um Market Maker in Echtgeld-Prognosemärkten zu betreiben, d.h. zu subventionieren.

Hierzu wird in Beitrag #2 analysiert, mit wie viel Geld erstens ein Markt *maximal* subventioniert werden muss und zweitens, wie hoch dieser erwartete Betrag *im Schnitt* ausfällt. Anders als in Beitrag #1 werden hier nicht alle vier verschiedenen Market Maker untersucht, sondern nur diejenigen, die schon durch ihren Aufbau eine obere Grenze für anfallende Kosten besitzen, nämlich die Logarithmic Scoring Rules (LMSR) und der Dynamic Parti-Mutuel Market (DPM).

Zunächst werden im Beitrag die oberen Grenzen für die Subventionen durch Analyse der Struktur der Market Marker hergeleitet. Diese werden durch einen einzigen Parameter, der auch die Schnelligkeit der Preisänderungen im Markt und damit die Prognosegüte beeinflusst, gesteuert. Auch hier werden, wie in Beitrag #1, die Evaluationen durch Simulationen durchgeführt. Allerdings werden hier zusätzlich Daten aus einem Echtgeld-Prognosemarkt als Datengrundlage verwendet, die es erlauben, Aussagen über die absolute Höhe der Subventionen abzuleiten.

Die Simulationen zeigen, dass nach der Bestimmung der optimalen Parameterwerte die theoretisch höchsten nötigen Subventionen, die analytisch bestimmt werden können, beim DPM auftreten können; die theoretisch höchsten Subventionen sind beim LMSR wesentlich geringer. Eine Analyse der tatsächlich auftretenden Subventionen mit Hilfe der Simulationsdaten zeigt allerdings, dass die theoretischen Subventionen beim DPM weitaus höher sind, als sie in den Märkten auftreten. Für 100 Handelsperioden kann hier festgestellt werden, dass die maximalen Subventionen beim DPM 7,35 € betragen, beim LMSR 13,75 €. Bei den durchschnittlichen Subventionen ist das Bild ähnlich, hier werden beim DPM 1,50 € benötigt, beim LMSR 3,66 €. Es kann weiterhin gezeigt werden, dass sowohl die maximalen als auch die durchschnittlichen Subventionen bei beiden Market Makern ungefähr linear mit der Anzahl der Handelperioden verlaufen.

Beitrag #2 zeigt also, dass erstens der DPM in Bezug auf die auftretenden nötigen Subventionen Vorteile gegenüber dem LMSR bietet. Auf der anderen Seite sind die Subventionen auch beim LMSR nicht sonderlich hoch, so dass der Einsatz dieser Market Maker eine realistische Alternative zu kontinuierlichen doppelten Auktionen darstellt, was damit auch deren Einsatz in Echtgeld-Prognosemärkten durchführbar erscheinen lässt. Betreiber können mit Hilfe dieses Beitrages also abschätzen, wie viel Geld sie für den Einsatz eines

Market Makers in Abhängigkeit der gewählten Parametrisierung aufbringen müssten und so entscheiden, ob ein Einsatz mit Spiel- oder Echtgeld für sie vorteilhafter ist.

I.3.3. Second-Generation Prediction Markets for Information Aggregation: A Comparison of Payoff Mechanisms

Obwohl Prognosemärkte der „ersten Generation" stets sehr gute Prognosegüten zeigen, haben sie doch eine gravierende Einschränkung: Prognosen können nur für Ereignisse ermittelt werden, die kurz- oder mittelfristig eintreten, um die Aktienauszahlung, d.h. den Wert der Aktie am Ende des Marktes, zu bestimmen. Viele betriebswirtschaftliche Entscheidungen basieren allerdings auf Ereignissen, die entweder nie oder erst in langem Zeitabstand eintreten. Beispiele hierfür sind die Auswahl zwischen mehreren Alternativen wie Produktkonzepten, von denen nur eine Teilmenge implementiert wird oder bewertet werden kann, oder aber strategische Entscheidungen, deren Erfolg erst spät, d.h. in einigen Jahren, gemessen werden kann (Dahan et al., 2009, Graefe und Weinhardt, 2008).

Um diese Einschränkung zu umgehen, zeigen bestehende Studien mit Prognosemärkten der „zweiten Generation", dass nicht unbedingt kurz- und mittelfristig eintretende Ereignisse für die Durchführung der Prognosemärkte notwendig sind, sondern dass sich die Auszahlung der Aktien auch an den im Markt entstehenden Daten anlehnen kann (Chan et al., 2002, Dahan et al., 2009, LaComb et al., 2007, Soukhoroukova und Spann, 2005). Hierbei werden insgesamt drei verschiedene Auszahlungsmechanismen vorgeschlagen (basierend auf dem volumengewichteten durchschnittlichen Preis der letzten Handelsphase, auf dem letzten Handelspreis mit festem Marktschluss und auf dem letzten Handelspreis mit zufälligem Marktschluss). Es gibt allerdings keinerlei Aussagen darüber, welcher der Mechanismen zur höchsten Prognosequalität führt. Weiterhin ist nicht bekannt, wie gut die Ergebnisse der Prognosemärkte der „zweiten Generation" in Relation zu einem Benchmark, der die optimale Aggregationsform darstellt, überhaupt sind.

Daher ist es Ziel des Beitrags #3, den „besten" Auszahlungsmechanismus, d.h. denjenigen mit der höchsten Prognosequalität, zu identifizieren. Hierzu werden in einem ersten Schritt die drei Mechanismen konzeptionell miteinander verglichen und ihre Auswirkungen auf das Handelsverhalten der Teilnehmer diskutiert. Es stellt sich heraus, dass theoretisch alle Märkte mit alternativen Auszahlungsmechanismen eine weitaus niedrigere Prognosequalität erreichen sollten als die der Prognosemärkte der „ersten Generation" mit Auszahlungen basierend auf dem Ausgang des Ereignisses. Auch bezüglich des Handelsverhaltens sollten alle alternativen Mechanismen Nachteile, d.h. Verzerrungen, gegenüber dem Benchmark besitzen.

Diese konzeptionellen Überlegungen werden anschließend in einem Feldexperiment mit insgesamt 78 MBA-Studenten an der University of Maryland, USA, getestet. Um die externe Validität zu bestimmen, werden die Prognosen auf kurzfristig eintretende Ereignisse angewendet. Hierbei werden mit Politik, Sport und Wirtschaft drei verschiedene Themen von Ereignissen getestet, da diese Einfluss auf die Prognosegüte bei verschiedenen Marktdesigns haben können (Rosenbloom und Notz, 2006). Als Marktmechanismus kommen die in Beitrag #1 als bester Mechanismus identifizierten Logarithmic Market Scoring Rules zum Einsatz.

Die Ergebnisse zeigen, dass bezüglich der Prognosegüte diejenigen Märkte am besten abschneiden, die den letzten gehandelten Preis als Auszahlung haben. Insgesamt ist hier die Prognosegüte nur 4,4 Prozentpunkte schlechter als bei den Prognosemärkten der ersten Generation, dem Benchmark. Ein Regressionsmodell, das auch den Aktientyp und die verschiedenen Themen beinhaltet, zeigt, dass die Prognosen sogar insignifikant verschieden sind. Obwohl der letzte Preismechanismus der beste ist, sind die beiden anderen Mechanismen auch nur maximal 1,7 Prozentpunkte schlechter als dieser.

Beim Handelsverhalten über die Zeit kann gezeigt werden, dass sich die Märkte mit den alternativen Auszahlungsmechanismen sowohl bezüglich der Preise als auch der Anzahl der gehandelten Aktien bis wenige Stunden vor Marktende nicht signifikant unterscheiden. Signifikante Unterschiede gibt es bei den Märkten mit Auszahlungen basierend auf einem volumengewichteten durchschnittlichen Preis nur gegen Ende. Erstaunlicherweise kann auch kein „last minute"-Handeln bei dem Markt mit Auszahlung basierend auf dem letzten Preis festgestellt werden.

Der Beitrag #3 zeigt somit, dass Prognosemärkte der „zweiten Generation" trotz ihrer konzeptionellen Schwächen relativ valide Instrumente in der Anwendung sind, um Informationen zu aggregieren, mit einem Abstand von 4,4 Prozentpunkten gegenüber Prognosemärkten der „ersten Generation". Bezüglich der Prognosegüte unterscheiden sich die Auszahlungsmechanismen hier nur minimal, womit es für Betreiber weitestgehend unerheblich ist, welchen Auszahlungsmechanismus sie zu Grunde legen.

I.3.4. An Empirical Investigation of the Forecast Accuracy of Play-Money Prediction Markets and Professional Betting Markets

Die Prognosegüte von Prognosemärkten ist sehr hoch gegenüber alternativen Instrumenten wie Befragungen (Berg et al., 2008), Expertenmeinungen (Spann und Skiera, 2003, Pennock et al., 2001) oder offiziellen Firmenprognosen (Chen und Plott, 2002, Ortner, 2000). Die empirischen Vergleiche von Prognosemärkten mit oben genannten Instrumenten sind möglicherweise aus praktischer Sicht gerechtfertigt, doch wird bei keinem dieser Instrumente der Anreiz gegeben, dass Teilnehmer ihre möglichst wahren Einschätzungen preisgeben. So werden beispielsweise Experten für falsche oder richtige Prognosen weder bestraft noch belohnt (Sunstein, 2006). Hier bleibt also immer noch die Frage offen, wie Prognosemärkte, vor allem diejenigen mit Spielgeldeinsatz, bezüglich Prognosegüte gegenüber Instrumenten abschneiden, die starke Anreize bieten, möglichst genaue Prognosen zu treffen.

Zur Klärung dieser Frage wird im Beitrag #4 die Prognosegüte eines durch Kooperation mit der Universität Karlsruhe entwickelten und betriebenen Spielgeld-Prognosemarktes *STOCCER* (www.stoccer.com) zur Fußball-Weltmeisterschaft 2006 mit den Prognosen professioneller Wettanbieter verglichen. Zusätzlich werden auch noch Vergangenheitsdaten aus einem FIFA-Ranking und einer Zufallsziehung zum Vergleich herangezogen. Hierbei haben Wettanbieter, die feste Quoten für Spielausgänge anbieten, einen extrem hohen Anreiz, gute Prognosen zu generieren, da sie ansonsten langfristig finanzielle Verluste hinnehmen müssten (Forrest et al., 2005). Es steht also für die Wettanbieter im Vergleich eine sehr hohe Summe auf dem Spiel, während es bei den Spielgeld-Prognosemärkten keine Möglichkeit für Verluste gibt. Folglich sollte der Anreiz, gut zu prognostizieren, bei Wettanbietern klar am höchsten sein.

Im Prognosemarkt STOCCER werden zwei Arten von Märkten analysiert: ein Turniermarkt, bei dem auf den Ausgang des Turniers spekuliert wird, und einzelne Spielmärkte für jedes der 16 Finalspiele. Im Schnitt werden 1600 Transaktionen pro Tag ausgeführt. Zwei professionelle, voneinander unabhängige Wettanbieter werden als Vergleich genutzt. Bei einem Anbieter ist der Wetteinsatz für das Jahr 2006 bekannt und liegt bei über 300 Millionen Euro, davon ein Großteil im Zusammenhang mit der Fußball-Weltmeisterschaft 2006. Das FIFA-Ranking beinhaltet eine Historie über acht Jahre und enthält mehrere Faktoren wie Ergebnis der Spiele oder Stärke der Gegner. Bei der Zufallsziehung werden Sieg,

Niederlage oder Unentschieden (d.h. Gleichstand nach 90 Minuten) als gleich wahrscheinlich angenommen (Schmidt und Werwatz, 2002).

Die Evaluation zeigt, dass die Prognosegüte des Turniermarktes, gemessen als Anteil der richtig prognostizierten Spielausgänge (Sieg, Niederlage oder Unentschieden), zwar leicht unter denen der Wettanbieter liegt (mit 9,5% bzw. 11,6% schlechterer Trefferquote der Spiele), die Ergebnisse sich aber nicht signifikant unterscheiden. Trotz der leicht schlechteren Quote ist die Prognosegüte dennoch überraschend hoch für den Spielgeld-Prognosemarkt. Dies gilt vor allem, wenn man bedenkt, dass die Wahrscheinlichkeit von Unentschieden bzw. Torgleichstand nach 90 Minuten bei dem Turniermarkt untergewichtet wird, da dort Preisgleichheit der Aktien hätte herrschen müssen. Gegenüber dem FIFA-Ranking kann eine signifikant höhere Verbesserung (26,7%) der Trefferquote des Prognosemarktes festgestellt werden, ebenso gegenüber der Zufallsziehung (78,1%).

Die 16 Spielmärkte zeigen allerdings sowohl gegenüber dem Turniermarkt als auch gegenüber den Wettanbietern bessere, wenn auch nicht signifikante Resultate. Während bei den letzten 16 Spielen die Trefferquote des Turniermarktes gleich der der Wettanbieter ist, weisen die Spielmärkte eine fast 43% bessere Prognosegüte auf. Ein möglicher Grund hierfür ist, dass in dem Turniermarkt Teilnehmer auch nachfolgende Spiele mit einrechnen, während sie sich bei den Spielmärkten auf ein einziges Spiel beschränken können. Die Spielmärkte schneiden auch wiederum gegenüber FIFA-Ranking und Zufallsziehung signifikant besser ab.

Beitrag #4 zeigt also, dass Spielgeld-Prognosemärkte eine sehr hohe Prognosegüte haben, trotz der fehlenden monetären Anreize im Vergleich zu Wettanbietern. Dieses Ergebnis ist vor allem vor dem Hintergrund zu sehen, dass Wettanbieter in der Vergangenheit bereits sehr gute Prognosegüten demonstriert haben (Pope und Peel, 1989). Während in einer früheren Studie schon gezeigt wurde, dass Echtgeld-Prognosemärkte so gut wie Wettanbieter prognostizieren (Schmidt und Werwatz, 2002), kann hier gezeigt werden, dass auch Spielgeld-Prognosemärkte gute Prognosen liefern. Dieses Ergebnis ist insbesondere interessant, da im Allgemeinen nach derzeitiger Rechtslage zumindest in Deutschland Spielgeldmärkte wesentlich einfacher zu implementieren und durchzuführen sind.

I.3.5. Event Studies in Real- and Play-Money Prediction Markets

Ereignisstudien mit Finanzmarktdaten öffentlich gelisteter Unternehmen sind heute weithin als Standardinstrument akzeptiert, um den Wert eines Ereignisses, wie z.B. die Einführung eines neuen Produktes (Chaney et al., 1991), als Änderung der Marktkapitalisierung zu quantifizieren (z.B. Khotari und Warner, 2006, MacKinlay, 1997). Um den Wert eines Ereignisses zu messen, muss allerdings ein geeignetes Wertpapier auf dem Finanzmarkt gehandelt werden. Zudem muss das Ereignis einen signifikanten Einfluss auf die Aktienpreise bzw. -renditen besitzen. Sollte eine dieser Voraussetzungen nicht erfüllt sein, bspw. bei Ereignissen mit weniger starken Auswirkungen, so können theoretisch auch Prognosemärkte als Datenquelle für Ereignisstudien dienen. Trotz dieser neuen und erfolgversprechenden Anwendung wurde bislang jedoch nicht analysiert, ob sich Prognosemärkte überhaupt für Ereignisstudien eignen und ob sich Unterschiede beim Einsatz von Spiel- und Echtgeld ergeben.

Um diese Fragen zu beantworten, wird in Beitrag #5 auf die Transaktionsdaten von zwei großen Prognosemärkten der Fußball-Europameisterschaft 2004 zurückgegriffen. Fußballdaten bieten gegenüber anderen Daten den großen Vorteil, dass erstens störende Ereignisse identifiziert und ausgeschlossen werden können und zweitens Ereignisse unvorhergesehen auftreten (Voraussetzungen für Ereignisstudien nach McWilliams und Siegel, 1997). Im Beitrag werden zunächst Modelle analysiert, wie in Finanzmärkten erwartete Renditen von Aktien berechnet werden, die dann mit den tatsächlichen Renditen unter Einfluss des Ereignisses verglichen werden können. Es kann gezeigt werden, dass in den meisten Prognosemärkten auf Grund der Abhängigkeit einzelner Aktien untereinander nur das simple Modell der konstanten durchschnittlichen Renditen angewandt werden kann.

Nach Auswertung von insgesamt 42 nach McWilliams und Siegel (1997) ausgewählten Toren als Ereignisse können als empirische Ergebnisse eine Reihe von Aussagen getroffen werden. Bezüglich der Höhe und Stabilität der kumulierten abnormalen, d.h. nicht erwarteten, Renditen, zeigen beide Prognosemärkte klare und stabile Reaktionen auf Ereignisse. So werden für positive Ereignisse, d.h. Tore der eigenen Mannschaft, positive abnormale Renditen erwartet, bei negativen Ereignissen, d.h. Gegentoren, entsprechend negative Renditen. Als zweiten Aspekt der Evaluation kann durch eine Analyse der Perioden mit signifikant abnormalen Renditen gezeigt werden, dass das Ereignis bei dem Echtgeld-Prognosemarkt im Schnitt in einer Minute und acht Sekunden verarbeitet ist, während die

Verarbeitung bei den Spielgeldmärkten mit einer Minute und 22 Sekunden signifikant länger dauert. Weiterhin wird bei beiden Prognosemärkten gezeigt, dass die Prognosefehler sich durch Anpassen der Kurse nach einem Ereignis signifikant verringern. Schließlich wird gezeigt, dass der Echtgeld-Prognosemarkt signifikant weniger liquide ist als der Spielgeld-Prognosemarkt, was sowohl die Anzahl der Händler (50% weniger) als auch die Anzahl der Transaktionen pro Spiel (59% weniger) anbelangt.

Beitrag #5 zeigt somit, dass sich Prognosemärkte für Ereignisstudien eignen und legt so die Grundlage für neue Anwendungsgebiete von Prognosemärkten. Auch stellt sich heraus, dass es, zumindest bei den vorliegenden Datensätzen, keine größeren Unterschiede bezüglich der Stabilität sowie der Schnelligkeit und Verbesserung der Prognosegüte der Ereignisreaktion gibt. Erklärt werden kann dieses Ergebnis durch die Tatsache, dass durch die festgestellte erhöhte Liquidität im Spielgeld-Prognosemarkt die Transaktionen der potenziell uninformierten Teilnehmer (Gruca et al., 2003) durch die Transaktionen informierter Teilnehmer ausgeglichen werden können. Zudem funktioniert die Ereignisstudie bei Echtgeld-Prognosemärkten durch das potenzielle Fehlen uninformierter Teilnehmer auch bei weniger liquiden Prognosemärkten. Mit diesem Beitrag werden Prognosemärkte also als Datenquelle erschlossen, mit der sich der „Wert" von Ereignissen mit kleinerer Auswirkung messen lassen kann, der nichtsdestotrotz wichtige Informationen über das Ereignis enthalten kann (Elberse, 2007). Neben Ereignissen mit relativ kleiner Auswirkung ist es nun möglich, Prognosemärkte speziell für bestimmte Ereignisse aufzusetzen, die man unabhängig von anderen, eventuell gleichzeitig auftretenden Ereignissen durch Ereignisanalyse bewerten kann.

I.4. Fazit und Ausblick

Innovative Anwendungen und neue Vorschläge zum Design von Prognosemärkten sind in der Forschung und Praxis immer häufiger anzutreffen, allerdings selten bis nie mit entsprechender Evaluation der Effektivität und Bestimmung des optimalen Designs. In dieser kumulativen Dissertation werden mit fünf Beiträgen grundlegende Aspekte des Designs von Prognosemärkten und Marktmechanismen im Allgemeinen sowie im Rahmen der Anwendung von Prognosemärkten sowohl der „ersten" als auch „zweiten Generation" untersucht. Dadurch werden Erkenntnisse für die Theorie gewonnen sowie Empfehlungen für die Praxis abgeleitet. Um dies zu erreichen, wird auf eine breite Palette an Methoden (mikroökonomische Modellierung, Simulationsstudie, Feldexperiment, Ereignisstudie) zurück gegriffen, um so die geeignetste zur Erreichung des jeweiligen Ziels anzuwenden. Diese Dissertation liefert somit Hilfestellung bezüglich der Auswahl zwischen bestehenden Ausprägungen von Designparametern und ermöglicht zudem die Quantifizierung der resultierenden Güte.

Von der theoretischen Seite wird im Themenkomplex der Marktmechanismen (Beiträge #1 und #2) gezeigt, welches die Funktionsweisen der Mechanismen sind und welche Auswirkungen diese Funktionsweisen auf die Effektivität in mehreren Dimensionen besitzen. Zudem wird durch das entwickelte, allgemeine Modell für die Simulationen die Möglichkeit der Evaluation für nachfolgende Marktmechanismen gegeben. Im Themenkomplex der Anwendungen zeigt die Dissertation, dass Prognosemärkte trotz möglicher Schwächen, nämlich fehlende Ausgänge von Ereignissen und dadurch möglicherweise falschem Anreiz für Teilnehmer (Beitrag #3) oder geringem ökonomischen Anreiz für Teilnehmer (Beitrag #4), vergleichbar gute Ergebnisse liefern. Beitrag #5 zeigt zudem erstmals, dass Preise in Prognosemärkten nicht nur an einem Punkt, sondern auch über die Zeit effizient sind.

Für die Praxis wird in dieser Dissertation mit den Beiträgen #1 und #2 eine detaillierte Entscheidungshilfe gegeben, mit welchen Marktmechanismen verschiedene Ziele erreicht werden können und welche Eigenschaften diese Mechanismen besitzen. Beitrag #3 belegt die Effektivität der Prognosemärkte der zweiten Generation und lässt so eine genau quantifizierbare Aussage über die Prognosegüte zu. Beitrag #4 gibt Praktikern einen Nachweis der guten Prognosegüte von Spielgeldmärkten, sogar im Vergleich zu Instrumenten, die in der Theorie möglicherweise besser vorhersagen sollten. Beitrag #5 erschließt letztendlich eine komplett neue Anwendungsmöglichkeit von Prognosemärkten und zeigt, dass mit der Messung von Preisreaktionen auf Ereignisse auch eine Bewertung der Ereignisse effektiv erfolgen kann.

Zukünftige Forschungsarbeiten können an jedem der zwei in dieser Dissertation behandelten Themenkomplexe ansetzen. Bezüglich der Marktmechanismen ist es sowohl für die Forschung als auch für die Praxis sicherlich ein sehr interessantes Thema, wie Prognosen nicht nur als Mittelwert, sondern auch als Verteilung der erwarteten Werte um den Prognosepunkt herum mit dem geeigneten Marktmechanismus modelliert werden können. Dies würde Praktikern die große Hilfe geben, zu bestimmen, wie sicher eine Prognose ist und wie wahrscheinlich Abweichungen von dieser sind. Erste Ansätze finden sich bereits in den Märkten von „Yoopick" (sandbox.yahoo.net/Yoopick, Goel et al., 2008).

Bezüglich der Anwendungen sind verschiedene offene Themen erkennbar. Offensichtlich hat der offene Quadrant rechts unten in Abbildung 2, bei dem es um die weitergehende Datennutzung bei Prognosemärkten der „zweiten Generation" geht, großes Potenzial. Hier sind Anwendungen vorstellbar, bei denen Szenarien an einem Prognosemarkt „gespielt" werden könnten, um so die Reaktion der Aktienpreise auf fiktive Ereignisse, z.b. Wettbewerbsaktionen, zu messen (Dahan et al., 2009). Der Vorteil von Prognosemärkten gegenüber anderen Instrumenten ist hier wiederum mit der Skalierbarkeit z.b. bezüglich der Anzahl der Teilnehmer oder der Aktien, den entstehenden Kosten und dem Aggregationsmechanismus gegeben.

Literaturverzeichnis

Berg, J., Forsythe, R., Nelson, F. & Rietz, T. (2003) Results from a Dozen Years of Election Futures Markets Research. In Plott, C. & Smith, V. (Eds.) *Handbook of Experimental Economic Results.* Amsterdam, Elsevier.

Berg, J. E., Nelson, F. D. & Rietz, T. A. (2008) Prediction Market Accuracy in the Long Run. *International Journal of Forecasting,* 24 (2), 285-300.

Chan, N., Dahan, E., Kim, A., Lo, A. & Poggio, T. (2002) Securities Trading of Concepts (STOC). Arbeitspapier, Massachusetts Institute of Technology.

Chaney, P. K., Devinney, T. M. & Winer, R. (1991) The Impact of New Product Introductions on the Market Value of Firms. *Journal of Business,* 64 (4), 573-610.

Chen, K.-Y. & Plott, C. R. (2002) Information Aggregation Mechanisms: Concept, Design and Implementation for a Sales Forecasting Problem. Arbeitspapier, California Institute of Technology.

Christiansen, J. D. (2007) Prediction Markets: Practical Experiments in Small Markets and Behaviours Observed. *Journal of Prediction Markets,* 1 (1), 17–41.

Dahan, E., Soukhoroukova, A. & Spann, M. (2009) New Product Development 2.0: Preference Markets — How Scalable Securities Markets Identify Winning Product Concepts & Attributes. *Journal of Product Innovation Management, erscheint.*

Elberse, A. (2007) The Power of Stars: Do Star Actors Drive the Success of Movies? *Journal of Marketing,* 71 (4), 102-120.

Fama, E. F. (1970) Efficient Capital Markets: A Review of Theory and Empirical Work. *Journal of Finance*, 25 (2), 383-417.

Fama, E. F. (1991) Efficient Capital Markets: II. *Journal of Finance*, 46 (5), 1575-1617.

Forrest, D., Goddard, J. & Simmons, R. (2005) Odds-Setters as Forecasters: The Case of English Football. *International Journal of Forecasting*, 21 (3), 551-564.

Forsythe, R., Nelson, F., Neumann, G. R. & Wright, J. (1992) Anatomy of an Experimental Political Stock Market. *American Economic Review*, 82 (5), 1142-1161.

Forsythe, R., Rietz, T. A. & Ross, T. W. (1999) Wishes, Expectations and Actions: A Survey on Price Formation in Election Stock Markets. *Journal of Economic Behavior & Organization*, 39 (1), 83-110.

Foutz, N. & Jank, W. (2008) The Wisdom of Crowds: Pre-release Forecasting via Functional Shape Analysis of the Online Virtual Stock Market. Arbeitspapier, University of Maryland.

Geyer-Schulz, A., Luckner, S., Schröder, J., Skiera, B., Slamka, C. & Weinhardt, C. (2007) An Empirical Evaluation of Call Auctions in Prediction Markets. Arbeitspapier, Universität Karlsruhe (TH).

Glosten, L. R. & Milgrom, P. R. (1985) Bid, Ask and Transaction Prices in a Specialist Market With Heterogeneously Informed Traders. *Journal of Financial Economics*, 14 (1), 71-100.

Goel, S., Pennock, D., Reeves, D. M. & Yu, C. (2008) Yoopick: A Combinatorial Sports Prediction Market. *Proceedings of the Twenty-Third AAAI Conference on Artificial Intelligence*.

Graefe, A. (2008) Prediction Markets – Defining Events and Motivating Participation. *Foresight*, 9, 30-32.

Graefe, A. & Weinhardt, C. (2008) Long-term Forecasting with Prediction Markets — A Field Experiment on Applicability and Expert Confidence. *Journal of Prediction Markets*, 2 (2), 71-92.

Gruca, T. S., Berg, J. & Cipriano, M. (2003) The Effect of Electronic Markets on Forecasts of New Product Success. *Information Systems Frontiers*, 5 (1), 95-105.

Hanson, R. (2003) Combinatorial Information Market Design. *Information Systems Frontiers*, 5 (1), 107-119.

Hanson, R. (2007) Logarithmic Market Scoring Rules for Modular Combinatorial Information Aggregation. *Journal of Prediction Markets*, 1 (1), 3-15.

Hayek, F. A. v. (1945) The Use of Knowledge in Society. *American Economic Review*, 35 (4), 519-530.

Holden, C. (2007) Bird Flu Futures. *Science*, 315, 1345.

Keiser, T. M. & Burns, M. R. (1999) Computer-Implemented Securities Trading System with a Virtual Specialist Function. Vereinigte Staaten Patent Nummer 5,950,176, ausgestellt an HSX, Inc.

Keiser, T. M. & Burns, M. R. (2003) Computer-Implemented Securities Trading System with a Virtual Specialist Function. Vereinigte Staaten Patent Nummer 6,505,174 B1, ausgestellt an HSX, Inc.

Keiser, T. M. & Burns, M. R. (2006) Computer-Implemented Securities Trading System with a Virtual Specialist Function. Vereinigte Staaten Patent Nummer 7,006,991 B2, ausgestellt an CFPH, LL.C.

Khotari, S. P. & Warner, J. B. (2006) Econometrics of Event Studies. In Eckbo, B. E. (Ed.) *Handbook of Corporate Finance: Empirical Corporate Finance*. Elsevier/North-Holland.

LaComb, C. A., Barnett, J. A. & Pan, Q. (2007) The Imagination Market. *Information Systems Frontiers*, 9 (2-3), 245-256.

Luckner, S. (2008) Predictive Power of Markets. Dissertation, Universität Karlsruhe (TH).

Luckner, S. & Weinhardt, C. (2007) How to Pay Traders in Information Markets? Results from a Field Experiment. *Journal of Prediction Markets*, 1 (2), 1-10.

MacKinlay, C. M. (1997) Event Studies in Economics and Finance. *Journal of Ecomomic Literature*, 35 (3), 13-39.

McWilliams, A. & Siegel, D. (1997) Event Studies in Management Research: Theoretical and Empirical Issues. *The Academy of Management Journal*, 40 (3), 626-657.

Oliven, K. & Rietz, T. A. (2004) Suckers Are Born but Markets Are Made: Individual Rationality, Arbitrage, and Market Efficiency on an Electronic Futures Market. *Management Science*, 50 (3), 336-351.

Ortner, G. (1998) Forecasting Markets — An Industrial Application: Part I. Arbeitspaper, TU Wien.

Ortner, G. (2000) Aktienmärkte als Industrielles Vorhersagemodell. *Zeitschrift für Betriebswirtschaft - Ergänzungsheft*, 70 (1), 115-125.

Pennock, D. M. (2004) A Dynamic Pari-Mutuel Market for Hedging, Wagering, and Information Aggregation. *ACM Conference on Electronic Commerce.* New York.

Pennock, D. M., Lawrence, S., Giles, C. L. & Nielsen, F. Å. (2001) The Real Power of Artificial Markets. *Science,* 291 (5506), 987-988.

Pope, P. F. & Peel, D. A. (1989) Information, Prices and Efficiency in a Fixed-Odds Betting Market. *Economica,* 56 (223), 323-341.

Ramsay, J. O. & Silverman, B. W. (2005) *Functional Data Analysis,* New York, Springer.

Rosenbloom, E. S. & Notz, W. W. (2006) Statistical Tests of Real-Money versus Play-Money Prediction Markets. *Electronic Markets,* 16 (1), 63-69.

Schmidt, C. & Werwatz, A. (2002) How Well do Markets Predict the Outcome of an Event? The Euro 2000 Soccer Championships Experiment. *Discussion Papers on Strategic Interaction* Jena, Germany, Max Planck Institute for Research into Economic Systems.

Servan-Schreiber, E., Wolfers, J., Pennock, D. M. & Galebach, B. (2004) Prediction Markets: Does Money Matter? *Electronic Markets,* 14 (3), 243-251.

Soukhoroukova, A. & Spann, M. (2005) New Product Development with Internet-based Information Markets: Theory and Empirical Application. *13th European Conference on Information Systems (ECIS).* Regensburg.

Soukhoroukova, A. & Spann, M. (2006) Schlagwort: Informationsmärkte. *WIRTSCHAFTSINFORMATIK,* 48 (1), 61-64.

Soukhoroukova, A., Spann, M. & Skiera, B. (2008) Creating and Evaluating New Product Ideas with Idea Markets. Arbeitspapier, Universität Passau.

Spann, M., Ernst, H., Skiera, B. & Soll, J. H. (2009) Identification of Lead Users for Consumer Products via Virtual Stock Markets. *Journal of Product Innovation Management,* 26 (3), 322-335.

Spann, M. & Skiera, B. (2003) Internet-Based Virtual Stock Markets for Business Forecasting. *Management Science,* 49 (10), 1310-1326.

Spann, M. & Skiera, B. (2004) Einsatzmöglichkeiten virtueller Börsen in der Marktforschung. *Zeitschrift für Betriebswirtschaft,* 74 (EH2), 25-48.

Spann, M. & Skiera, B. (2009) Sports Forecasting: A Comparison of the Forecast Accuracy of Prediction Markets, Betting Odds and Tipsters. *Journal of Forecasting,* 28 (1), 55-77.

Spann, M., Soukhoroukova, A. & Skiera, B. (2006) Prognose von Marktentwicklungen anhand virtueller Börsen. In Herrmann, A. & Homburg, C. (Eds.) *Marktforschung: Methoden – Anwendungen – Praxisbeispiele, 3. Auflage.* Wiesbaden, Gabler.

Sunstein, C. R. (2006) Deliberation and Information Markets. In Hahn, W. & Tetlock, P. C. (Eds.) *Information Markets: A New Way of Making Decisions.* Washington D.C., AEI-Brookings Press.

Van Bruggen, G. H., Spann, M., Lilien, G. L. & Skiera, B. (2008) Institutional Forecasting: The Performance of Thin Virtual Stock Markets *ERIM Report Series, Erasmus University.*

Weinhardt, C., Holtmann, C. & Neumann, D. (2003) Market-Engineering. *Wirtschaftsinformatik,* 45 (6), 635-640.

Wolfers, J. & Zitzewitz, E. (2004) Prediction Markets. *Journal of Economic Perspectives,* 18 (2), 107-126.

Prediction Market Performance and Market Liquidity: A Comparison of Automated Market Makers

Christian Slamka[1], Bernd Skiera[1], Martin Spann[2]

[1] School of Business and Economics, Goethe-University Frankfurt, Germany
[2] Chair of Marketing and Innovation, University of Passau, Germany

Abstract

The use of prediction markets (PMs) for forecasting is emerging in many fields and attains mostly superior forecasting accuracy compared with other instruments. However, PM accuracy depends on its market design, including the choice of the market mechanism. Standard financial market mechanisms are not well suited for small, usually illiquid PMs. To avoid liquidity problems, automated market makers (AMMs) always offer buy and sell prices. However, no comparison exists that measures their relative performance. This article compares the performance of four documented AMMs conceptually and empirically using a simulation study and thereby demonstrates that no single AMM performs best on all performance criteria. Logarithmic scoring rules and the dynamic pari-mutuel market attain the highest forecasting accuracy, good robustness against parameter misspecification, and the ability to incorporate new information into prices. However, in contrast with an AMM that accumulates orders, they are prone to noisy trading, which makes them inappropriate in environments with high uncertainty about true share prices.

Keywords: Computational Intelligence and Information Management, prediction markets, forecasting, wisdom of the crowds

1. Introduction

Interest in and the use of prediction markets (PMs) as a forecasting tool has grown in the past decade. Such markets began as niche applications in the field of political forecasting (e.g. Forsythe et al., 1992) but have found further applications in areas such as sports (e.g. Servan-Schreiber et al., 2004) and business-related fields, including sales forecasting (Chen and Plott, 2002), new product concept evaluations (Soukhoroukova and Spann, 2005, Dahan et al., 2009), and even the generation and evaluation of ideas within companies (Soukhoroukova et al., 2009). Several studies show that in terms of accuracy, PMs are mostly superior to other, comparable forecasting techniques such as polls (Berg et al., 2001), official company forecasts (Chen and Plott, 2002), or experts (Spann and Skiera, 2003)—enough so that notable companies such as Google (Cowgill et al., 2008), Microsoft, Eli Lilly, and Hewlett Packard (Kiviat, 2004) have started to use PMs.

These examples reveal that PMs increasingly have gained acceptance, though they do not determine which market design is best. This gap in existing research is surprising, because a well designed market is absolutely essential for a PM to produce accurate forecasts (Spann and Skiera, 2003). Market operators must make choices about several design characteristics, including the contract design (Wolfers and Zitzewitz, 2004), incentive mechanisms (Luckner and Weinhardt, 2007), or the application of real- or play-money investments (Servan-Schreiber et al., 2004, Slamka et al., 2008); perhaps the most crucial parameter is the market mechanism.

The choice of market mechanism becomes especially critical in situations with low liquidity, which are more likely when the number of stocks is rather large and/or the number of participating traders is low. Early PMs contained few stocks and a rather high number of traders, but more recent applications in corporate forecasting and new product development feature many stocks and relatively fewer traders (Dahan et al., 2009). In these situations, market liquidity represents a central problem for applying PMs successfully, which may inhibit the application of a continuous double auction trading mechanism. A possible solution is an automated market maker (AMM), which provides unlimited market liquidity by always offering buy and sell prices.

In general, AMMs offer to buy and sell shares at any given point in time, creating unlimited liquidity in the market. However, unlike market makers in real financial markets,

AMMs are not human but rather are automated and rely on software, which means they must be parameterized correctly. Despite their importance and various designs, no existing research provides a thorough comparison of their applicability so that it is not clear what differences exist among AMMs and which one performs best.

Therefore, the goal of this study is to present, describe, and compare AMMs from a conceptual point of view and evaluate their performance using a simulation study. To measure performance, we focus on three criteria. First, we analyze the overall forecasting accuracy of share prices, or *price efficiency*, which reflects the best predictions that can be achieved. Second, an AMM should be *robust* against deviations that an operator can control, as well as against deviations, which an operator cannot control but that are caused by traders. The first deviation is a parameter misspecification, which means the parameters deviate from their optimal selection. In contrast, an operator cannot control for the deviation resulting from noisy trading by less than perfectly informed traders. Third, the *speed* at which new information appears, or when an event occurs, can be captured in market prices, which is important for measuring the "value" of an event (Elberse, 2007, Slamka et al., 2008).

We structure the remainder of this article as follows: In Section 2, we describe and conceptually compare the four mechanisms and illustrate their functions. Then we describe the market model we use for the simulations. In Section 4, we outline the design of the simulation study, followed by the results we have obtained. Finally, in Section 5, we draw some conclusions.

2. Market Mechanisms

The first market mechanisms used in PMs came from financial exchanges, such as the Xetra Exchange (www.xetra.com), and often employed continuous double auctions (CDAs) throughout their trading phases. In CDAs, traders submit orders with a chosen maximum quantity of shares, usually with a price limit, into the order book. If a matching order appears, the order gets executed immediately. Thus, trades can be executed among traders themselves on a continuous basis, if enough liquidity, that is, orders, is present (Madhavan, 1992).

However, even in financial markets, liquidity may fall too low for sufficient trading activity, in which case market makers (MMs) enable trading. These MMs are professional, human traders who are willing and obliged to buy and sell shares of stock at predetermined prices (Krahnen and Weber, 2001, Madhavan, 2000). For example, the NASDAQ (www.nasdaq.com) uses such a trading system, which ensures virtually unlimited liquidity in the market.

The concepts of CDAs and MMs appear in PMs as well. As one of the most prominent and earliest examples, the Iowa Electronic Markets (Forsythe et al., 1999), also use CDAs in their exchange. Although illiquidity may be present in financial markets, the problem tends to be much more severe in PMs. In small, often company internal PMs, the number of traders is very low, and the number of stocks per trader is very high, which leads to a "chicken and egg problem": Traders are attracted to liquid markets, with high trading frequency, but liquid markets require many traders (Pennock, 2004). Fewer traders and trades lead to unreliable and inefficient market predictions, because fewer assessments by fewer traders regarding a forecasted event's outcome appear reflected in the predictions.

Although in theory, (human) MMs might be employed in PMs, this approach generally is not feasible because of the costs to what is essentially a market research instrument. Most PMs therefore use automated market makers (AMMs), which set share prices according to an algorithm included within software (Hanson, 2003, Pennock, 2004). Both human MMs in financial markets and AMMs in PMs share the primary goal of adding liquidity to markets, but human MMs must meet more constraints in their trading actions than AMMs. For example, AMMs are not required to make profits or omit losses, as human MMs commonly must (Roll, 1984). In the long run, the inventory of human MMs should be approximately level (Garman, 1976), but such considerations do not play any role for AMMs.

2.1. Overview

To date, four documented AMMs have been employed in PMs. One of the most widely used (e.g., by Inkling, www.inkling.com; XPree, www.xpree.com; Washington Stock Exchange, www.thewsx.com) involves logarithmic market scoring rules (LMSR) introduced by Hanson (2003, 2007). The subsequent dynamic pari-mutuel market (DPM) by Pennock (2004) appeared in the (now closed) Yahoo! Tech Buzz game (Chen et al., 2008, Mangold et al., 2005) and AskMarkets (www.askmarkets.com).

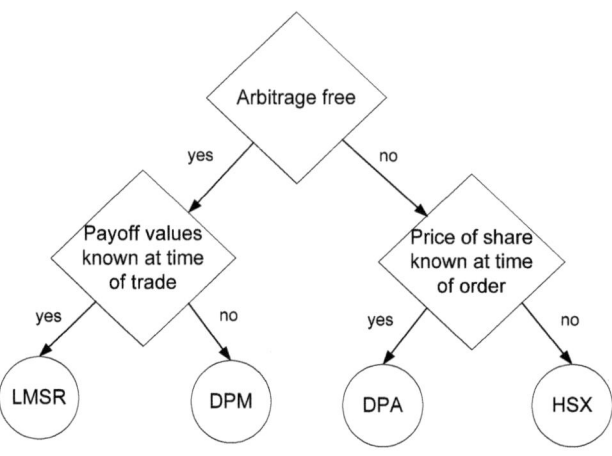

Figure 1: Main characteristics of analyzed market makers

Both LMSR and DPM maintain continuous price functions to determine share prices, which means they are arbitrage free (Figure 1). The price functions determine the share prices according to the number of shares present in the market. Because the price function is continuous, every purchased (sold) share is more (less) expensive per share. That is, the prices of shares are not fixed for single trades, as they are in two other AMM cases. Therefore, the purchase costs per share for ten shares will be higher than the corresponding costs for five shares. Each trade of several shares can be thought of as several trades of one share, and each purchase or sale has a higher or lower price than the previous one. Whereas the possible payoff values are known with LMSR, in DPM, the final payoff values are not known, because they depend on further market trading actions.

Two academic studies (Soukhoroukova et al., 2009, Van Bruggen et al., 2008) introduce an AMM that offers fixed purchase and sale prices of shares, which we call dynamic price adjustment (DPA). Finally, a prominent AMM is that used by the Hollywood Stock Exchange (HSX, www.hsx.com), the largest existing PM with several hundred thousand traders. Its underlying AMM has been described in three patents (Keiser and Burns 1999, 2003, 2006). Neither DPA nor HSX implements a continuous price function. Whereas the final price of a share is known to the trader at the time of the order in the DPA mechanism, it is not in the HSX.

2.2. Functionality of Mechanisms

In this subsection, we describe each AMM and complement our descriptions with three simple trading actions for each AMM, which we detail in the Appendix.

2.2.1 (Logarithmic) Market Scoring Rules

Market scoring rules (MSR), as the general concept behind LMSR, build on the long standing concept of scoring rules, which can evaluate a forecaster's performance (Winkler, 1969, DeGroot and Fienberg, 1983, O'Carroll, 1977). With simple scoring rules, forecasters give isolated, one time predictions, whereas Hanson's (Hanson, 2003, Hanson, 2007) MSR requires them to offer successive predictions about a particular forecasting goal by adjusting the most recent prediction. With an underlying continuous price function that depends on the particular scoring rule used, this AMM determines the price for each share sold or bought.

MSRs work with a set of N mutually exclusive and exhaustive outcomes, and the probabilities of all these outcomes sum to 1. The cost function $C(\vec{q_t})$, as the integral of the price function, reflects the amount of money already been spent on buying or selling $|\vec{q_t}| = \sum_{j=1}^{N} |q_{j,t}|$ shares, where $\vec{q_t} = (q_{1,t}, q_{2,t}, ..., q_{N,t})$ is the vector of the number of shares on the market after the tth trade in the market (Pennock and Sami, 2007). The amount of money that a trader must spend/receives for each trade is

$$(1) \quad Costs_{i,t}^{LMSR}\left(q_{i,t}^{current}\right) = C(\vec{q_t}) - C(\vec{q_{t-1}}) \text{ and } q_{i,t} - q_{i,t-1} = q_{i,t}^{current},$$

where $C(\vec{q_t})$ is the same vector as $C(\vec{q_{t-1}})$, except for one position i, which is the number of traded shares in transaction i, and a difference pertaining to the number of ordered shares of $q_{i,t}^{current}$. A trader who makes a purchase pays $C(\vec{q_t}) - C(\vec{q_{t-1}})$ if $q_{i,t}^{current} = q_{i,t} - q_{i,t-1} > 0$; one who makes a sale receives $C(\vec{q_{t-1}}) - C(\vec{q_t})$ if $q_{i,t}^{current} = q_{i,t} - q_{i,t-1} < 0$.

Although several scoring rules can represent MSRs, the logarithmic scoring rule has been applied widely. The cost function for LMSR is

(2) $$C(\vec{q_t}) = b \cdot \ln\left(\sum_{j \in N} \exp(q_{j,t}/b)\right).$$

Furthermore, MSRs require a subsidy b that determines the maximum amount of money an AMM can lose overall. It also controls liquidity in the market, such that a higher subsidy adds more liquidity to the market and lets prices move more slowly. The current price for an infinitesimally small amount of shares is the derivative of the cost function (equation (2)), and the price function is

(3) $$p_i(\vec{q_t}) = \frac{\exp(q_{i,t}/b)}{\sum_{j \in N} \exp(q_{j,t}/b)} = \pi_{i,t},$$

where $\pi_{i,t}$ is the probability that the ith stock's underlying event will occur after the tth trade in the case of a winner takes all market. Because this price quote is only valid for an infinitesimally small amount of shares, a trader that hopes to buy shares must pay more money per share than the current quote and receives less when selling shares. Because of the continuity of the price function, buying an arbitrary amount of shares and selling it again (or vice versa) will not lead to a change in a trader's portfolio value. Thus, this mechanism is arbitrage free.

2.2.2 Dynamic Pari-Mutuel Market

Standard pari-mutuel markets, known from horse races, can aggregate information efficiently at a single point in time (Snyder, 1978). At any time before the close of the market, money can be spent on each of the N mutually exclusive, exhaustive outcomes, such as the victory of a particular horse. After the close of the market, the total money spent on all possible outcomes is $M^{final} = \sum_{j \in N} m_j$, where m_j is the amount bet on outcome j. When the final outcome is known, each dollar invested in the "correct" event i is worth $\frac{M^{final}}{m_i} \geq \$1$. Despite their ability to aggregate information efficiently at the latest point in time, pari-mutuel markets cannot update predictions after the arrival of new information, such as news (Pennock, 2004).

The dynamic pari-mutuel market (DPM, Pennock, 2004) overcomes this problem by introducing dynamic prices for shares that represent the final amount of money, rather than maintaining a fixed price, as with the standard mechanism. Similar to MSRs, the price of a share depends on the number of shares in the market and the price function (Pennock and Sami, 2007). As in a standard pari-mutuel market, all money gets redistributed over all winning shares, and the price of a share does not correspond directly to actual probabilities in winner takes all markets but must be transformed into probabilities π (Chen et al., 2008):

(4) $$\pi_i(\vec{q_t}) = \frac{q_{i,t}^2}{\sum_{j \in N} q_{j,t}^2} = \pi_{i,t},$$

where $q_{i,t}$ is the number of shares of the ith stock on the market after the tth trade. The cost function then is defined as

(5) $$C(\vec{q_t}) = \sqrt{\sum_{j \in N} q_{j,t}^2},$$

which denotes a one to one mapping between the vector of the number of shares and the money in the market. When starting the market and to allow for trading, an initial amount $C(\vec{q_0}) = M^{ini}$ and a vector $\vec{q_0}$ of shares that contain positive quantities of shares of each stock must be assigned.[1]

Similar to the subsidy b with MSRs, the initial assignment of money/shares controls the liquidity of the market. The more seed money enters the market at the beginning, the slower the prices and implied probabilities move. Identical to MSRs, the cost of a trade equals the difference in the costs of the $(t-1)$th trade and the tth trade in the market, again using equation (1).

At the close of the market at time T, there are $|\vec{q_T}|$ shares on the market, and the corresponding money $C(\vec{q_T}) = M^{final}$ is totally invested. If the event that occurs out of the N events is i, all the money invested in all shares is equally split among the holders of that

---
[1] As with the MSR, we assume all N events to be equally likely, and thus, the elements of the initial vector of number of shares are equal.

share. That is, the value of the share of event i is $\dfrac{M^{final}}{q_{i,T}}$, where M^{final} denotes the total amount of money invested in all shares, including seed money, and $q_{i,T}$ is the number of shares of i at the close of the market. The price of an infinitesimal amount of shares in stock i is the derivative of the cost function (equation (5)), and the price function is

$$\text{(6)} \qquad p_i(\vec{q}_t) = \frac{q_{i,t}}{\sqrt{\sum_{j \in N} q_{j,t}^2}}.$$

In addition, the probabilities of events can be derived from not only the shares on the market (equation (4)) but also the share prices (Chen et al., 2008):

$$\text{(7)} \qquad \pi_i(\vec{q}_t) = \frac{p_{i,t}^2}{\sum_{j \in N} p_{j,t}^2} = \pi_{i,t}.$$

Because it uses a continuous price function, the DPM, as is the LMSR, is arbitrage free.

2.2.3 Dynamic Price Adjustment

In both LMSR and DPM, a continuous price function exists that determines the price of a share, depending on the order quantity. Another mechanism used in previous research (Van Bruggen et al., 2008, Soukhoroukova et al., 2009), the DPA, does not implement a continuous price function but rather offers an equal buy and sell price for each share of stock up to a certain maximum quantity. Thus, for $q_{i,t}^{current}$ shares of the ith stock at the tth trade of this particular stock, a trader pays or receives:

$$\text{(8)} \qquad Costs_{i,t}^{DPA}(q_{i,t}^{current}) = q_{i,t}^{current} \cdot p_{i,t-1},$$

where $p_{i,t-1}$ is the price of a share of the ith stock after the $(t-1)$st trade of this stock.

After the trade, a new price is calculated according to the last executed trades within a moving window. Therefore, after a purchase, the price rises, and even more so if the previous transactions also were purchases, because this trend indicates an increase in the underlying true value. The function for the price update of a share of stock i is given by (Van Bruggen et al., 2008):

$$(9) \quad p_{i,t}\left(p_{i,t-1}, \overrightarrow{q_{i,t}^{lag}}\right) = p_{i,t-1} + sign\left(q_{i,t,0}^{lag}\right) \cdot \max\left\{ \left|q_{i,t,0}^{lag}\right| \cdot \frac{p_{i,\max}^2}{\gamma^2} \cdot \frac{sig\left(q_{i,t,0}^{lag}\right) = sig\left(q_{i,t,k}^{lag}\right) \sum_{k=0}^{I_t} \left|q_{i,t,k}^{lag}\right|}{I_t + 1}, \tau \right\} = \pi_{i,t},$$

with $\overrightarrow{q_{i,t}^{lag}} = \left(q_{i,t,0}^{lag}, q_{i,t,1}^{lag}, \ldots, q_{i,t,I_t}^{lag}\right) = \left(q_{i,t}, q_{i,t-1}, q_{i,t-2}, \ldots, q_{i,t-I_t}\right), I_t = \begin{cases} t & \text{for } t < I \\ I & \text{for } t \geq I \end{cases}$, $|q_{i,n}| \leq q_{\max}$,

where:

$\overrightarrow{q_{i,t}^{lag}}$: vector of quantities of orders of shares of ith stock at the tth trade of the ith stock,

$q_{i,t}$: quantity of order of shares of ith stock at the tth trade of ith stock,

$p_{i,\max}$: maximum price for shares of ith stock,

I : length of moving average window,

γ: liquidity parameter ("gamma"),

τ : minimum tick size, and

$q_{\max}$: maximum number of tradable shares.

Thus, the higher the liquidity parameter γ the slower the share prices move. In contrast with LMSR and DPM, this market mechanism is not arbitrage free, so traders can buy shares of stock at a fixed price p^*, initiate a price update, and then sell it again for a price $p^{**} > p^*$, which nets them a profit of $p^{**} - p^*$ without risk. To avoid this situation in real-world applications, DPA requires a restriction that prevents a trader from executing opposing transactions with the same stock during a certain time frame.

2.2.4 (Basic) Hollywood Stock Exchange Mechanism

The Hollywood Stock Exchange (www.hsx.com) is one of the biggest PMs online and has not been described publicly in detail; however, the basic idea has been published in three patents (Keiser and Burns, 1999, Keiser and Burns, 2003, Keiser and Burns, 2006). During a certain time frame, or "sweep phase," for a specific stock, this mechanism collects buy and sell orders, comparable to call auctions in financial markets (Kehr et al., 2001), but does not execute them immediately. At the end of the sweep phase, it determines a net movement balance, which equals the difference in the number of shares of buy orders less the number of shares of sell orders. If this number is positive, demand for the shares of stock is higher than supply, which suggests a higher "true value" of the underlying shares.

The net movement balance then is multiplied by a scaling parameter, "alpha," to produce the projected price movement. The price movement may be attenuated by a "Virtual Specialist" function if it appears too strong.[2] The newly calculated price is the old price plus the price movement. At this point, the final buy/sell price for the ordered shares in the elapsed time frame can be calculated, and the user can be informed about the final buy or sell price.

Because we lack complete documentation, we refer to this AMM as the basic Hollywood Stock Exchange mechanism (bHSX) and rely on publicly available details. In this mechanism, the final buy and sell price for each share in the sth sweep phase is:

$$(10) \quad p_{i,s}\left(p_{i,s-1}, \overrightarrow{q_{i,s}^{sweep}}\right) = p_{i,s-1} + \alpha \cdot \sum_{z=1}^{|\overrightarrow{q_{i,s}^{sweep}}|} q_{i,s,z}^{sweep} = \pi_{i,s},$$

$$\text{with } q_{i,t} \in \overrightarrow{q_{i,s}^{sweep}} \text{ if } t-\text{th trade in } s-\text{th sweep\_phase}, \left|\sum_{z=1}^{|\overrightarrow{q_{i,s}^{sweep}}|} q_{i,s,z}^{sweep}\right| \leq q_{\max},$$

where:

$p_{i,s}$: final bHSX price for shares of the ith stock in the sth sweep phase for all trades in this phase,

$\overrightarrow{q_{i,s}^{sweep}}$: vector of quantities of orders of shares of ith stock in the sth sweep phase,

---

[2] Due to lack of documentation, we do not model the virtual specialist function.

$q_{i,t}$: quantity of order of shares of ith stock of tth trade,

I : length of sweep phase,

α : scaling parameter ("alpha"), and

q_{max} : maximum number of tradable shares.

For $q_{i,t}^{current}$ shares of the ith stock at the tth trade in the sth sweep phase, a trader pays or receives

(11) $$Costs_{i,t}^{bHSX}\left(q_{i,t}^{current}\right) = q_{i,t}^{current} \cdot p_{i,s}.$$

The higher the liquidity parameter alpha is, the faster the share prices move. Similar to the DPA, the (b)HSX is not arbitrage free, so losses potentially grow to infinity for the operators.

2.3. Comparison

We compare the mechanisms with respect to their general properties and usability for traders, implementation effort demanded of operators, and possible contract designs (Table 1).

	LMSR	DPM	DPA	(b)HSX
General properties				
Unlimited buy/sell liquidity	Yes	Yes	Yes	Yes
Immediate order execution	Yes	Yes	Yes	No
Price of shares dependent on money invested in markets/length of market	No	Yes	No	No
Arbitrage free	Yes	Yes	No	No
Usability				
Potential payoff values per share known at time of trade	Yes	No	Yes	Yes
Price of shares reflecting probabilities in case of winner takes all markets	Yes	No, to be transformed to probabilities	Yes	Yes
Final price of shares known to user before trade	Yes	Yes	Yes	No
Trading price of shares dependent on size of order	Yes	Yes	No	Yes, but not directly observable
Implementation effort				
Number of parameters to set	1	1	3	≥ 3
Monetary losses	Bounded	Bounded	Not bounded	Not bounded
Possible contract designs				
Winner takes all	Yes	Yes	Yes	Yes
Linear with prices/impl. probabilities of shares in market summing up to 1	Yes	Yes, with transformed	Yes	Yes
Linear in general	Yes	No	Yes	Yes

Table 1: Conceptual comparison of AMMs on general properties and usability

All AMMs provide unlimited buy and sell liquidity, which is their main advantage compared with other market mechanisms. However, LMSR, DPM, and DPA execute all orders immediately, whereas the HSX accumulates the orders during the sweep phase and executes them only at the end. In contrast with the other AMMs, the price of shares in the DPM depends on the money invested in the markets. Without continuous price functions, DPA and HSX are not arbitrage free, so traders might trade skillfully and outsmart the mechanism. Thus, these mechanisms require restraints to suppress such behavior, such as limiting the combination of subsequent purchases and sales.

Their main characteristics also affect the usability of the mechanisms. For example, in the DPM, the potential payoff values of each share are not known at the time of the trade, because they depend on the final amount of money and number of shares invested in the market. Therefore, if a trade is not the last one, a trader can only speculate about the final payoff value, which adds uncertainty to the investment decision. For the remaining AMMs, payoff values for each share are well defined and depend on the outcome of the event to be forecasted. Another drawback for the DPM's usability is that its share prices do not directly correspond to the probabilities in winner takes all markets. Therefore, a trader must explicitly or implicitly convert share prices to probabilities (see equation (4)) to make investment decisions. In contrast, share prices for LMSR, DPA, and HSX correspond to the probabilities.

A lack of knowledge of the final purchase or sale price of shares in the case of the HSX might be disadvantageous for traders, in that it adds uncertainty to the investment decision. In contrast, the DPA makes it very easy for traders: There is a single purchase and sale price, so traders base their decisions on just this price rather than incorporating a rising or falling price per share, depending on the number of bought or sold shares.

From a PM operator's point of view, a key criterion is the effort required to implement markets that run a specific AMM. The more parameters that must be set prior to running a market, the higher is the complexity and effort for the operator. Whereas LMSR and DPM require a single liquidity parameter, DPA and HSX need both liquidity parameters and lengths of the trading windows during which trades may be considered. The maximum number of tradable shares should be set in both AMMs. Moreover, whereas LMSR and DPM have strict bounds on losses, DPA and bHSX lack any such bounds, which is important in real-world markets. Losses for operators could grow to infinity in these latter cases, though this restraint takes minor importance in most play-money markets.

With regard to general applicability, the different possible contract designs for an AMM are critical (Wolfers and Zitzewitz, 2004, Spann and Skiera, 2003). All AMMs support so called winner takes all markets, in which a single winning share of stock cashes out at $1 in the case of LMSR, DPA, and HSX and $\frac{M^{final}}{q_{i,T}}$ in the case of DPM. The remaining shares cash out at $0. In linear contracts, shares of stock cash out between $0 and $1, and all share prices sum to $1. Thus, outcomes of elections might be forecast such that each party receives a share of p_i votes, and shares of stock i cashing out receives $\$p_i$ per share. In the case of the DPM, each share's cash out is $\frac{M^{final}}{q_{i,T}} \cdot p_i$, and all cash outs sum to M^{final}. In general, linear contracts, whose shares of stock can cash out at any value, are not supported by DPM, though LMSR can be designed to support this design (Hanson, 2003), and DPA and HSX both support it.

3. Simulation Study Design

3.1. Market Microstructure

The general idea of the evaluations in this section is to create a market environment that contains traders with certain properties, such as valuations, that are independent from any AMM (Figure 2). Then, by specifying the market model, we can determine how the shares are exchanged using a specific AMM, including the specific parameters. By keeping the market environment identical for all AMMs, we can measure the quality of the market outcome for each AMM and its parameter selection, which provides our market result. Deviations in the market results thus reflect the chosen AMMs and their selected parameters. This complete framework constitutes the market microstructure.

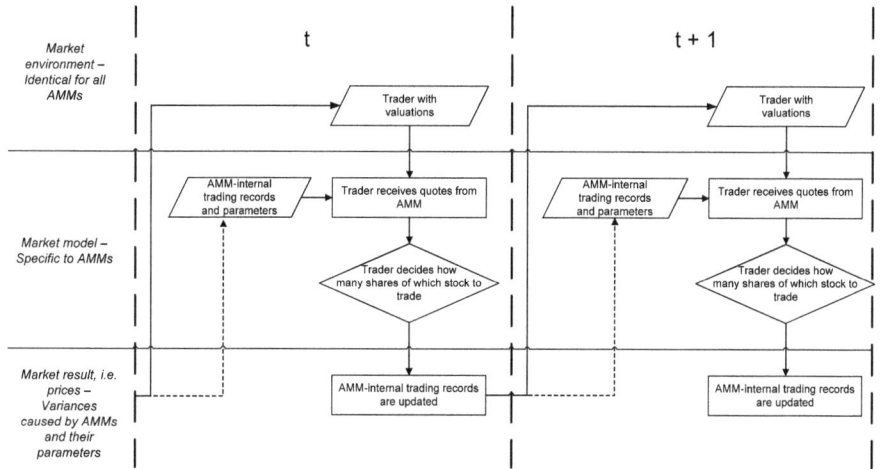

Figure 2: Overview of market microstructure

At a certain trading time t, a trader possesses valuations, which we describe in greater detail subsequently. The trader receives quotes from the AMM about decision relevant variables, such as share prices or the number of shares in the market. Using this information, the trader can decide which and how many shares of stock to trade. When the trader submits an order, the AMM internal trading records and prices get updated and new predictions are produced.

3.2. Model

As a basis for our simulations, we introduce a model that represents an extension of the model introduced by Das (2005), which itself is an extended version of Glosten and Milgrom's (1985) model. This extension is necessary to reflect the PM and AMM specific properties of the markets, such as the existence of two stocks in a market and varying order quantities rather than one stock or a fixed order quantity.

In Das's (2005) model, a stock i in the market exists whose shares can be traded only through the intermediation of a market maker; thus, one transaction side is always the MM, and the opposite side is always a trader. Traders in the market arrive one by one in discrete points in time $t \in \{1,...,T\}$ and may execute either buy or sell orders, or possibly no orders at all. The size of a trade is fixed to one unit for each trade, and in every period, the MM issues bid and ask prices for one unit, $P_{i,t,b}$ and $P_{i,t,a}$, respectively. The share of stock i has an underlying true value of $V_{i,t}$, which is exogenously given. In PMs, the true value may be the true probability that an event will occur (c.f. Wolfers and Zitzewitz, 2008). There are two types of risk neutral traders: perfectly informed traders that are aware of the share of stock's true value $V_{i,t}$ and noisy informed traders that receive a noisy signal $\omega(0, \sigma_{noisy})$ with a mean of 0 and a standard deviation of σ_{noisy}. More formally, a single trader at time t that trades the ith stock receives the following signal of the share of stock's valuation:

$$(12) \quad W_{i,t} = \begin{cases} V_{i,t}, & \text{if trader at time } t \text{ trading } i\text{th stock is perfectly informed,} \\ V_{i,t} + \omega(0, \sigma_{noisy}), & \text{if trader at time } t \text{ trading } i\text{th stock is noisy informed.} \end{cases}$$

As a consequence, a trader issues a sell order if $W_{i,t} < P_{i,t,b}$, such that a share of stock i at time t appears overvalued, or issues a buy order if $W_{i,t} > P_{i,t,a}$ for a (subjectively) undervalued share. If the signal lies within the spread, such that $P_{i,t,b} \leq W_{i,t} \leq P_{i,t,a}$, the trader issues no order.

Not all AMMs support all market designs, but both winner takes all and linear with shares in the market summing to 1 are supported by all markets; they are also the most prevalent designs. Therefore, in our extension, we assume two stocks, are present, and their shares' true values always add to 1, such that $V_{2,t} = 1 - V_{1,t}$ at all times t (cf. examples in Section 2.2). The true values of each share of stock, depending on the interpretation, reveal either the probability that a stock's underlying event will happen (winner takes all) or the expected value (linear) of the outcome (Spann and Skiera, 2003).

We assume all traders are aware of this property, which implies that we can deduce that the signal of the share of the second stock of a trader at time t, $W_{2,t}$, can be inferred by calculating $W_{2,t} = 1 - W_{1,t}$. Moreover, the choice of a buy or sell order is exogenous to the trader. If a buy order is chosen, the undervalued share (relative to $W_{i,t}$) is traded, whereas if a sell order is chosen, the overvalued share is traded. Because $V_{2,t} = 1 - V_{1,t}$ and $W_{2,t} = 1 - W_{1,t}$, it is unambiguous which share of stock is subjectively under-/overvalued or if the (transformed in DPM) share prices exactly correspond to the valuations, in which case no transaction occurs.

The second extension of the model aims to restrict the trading quantity to one share per period, though we suspend this restriction because different order quantities are essential for the price movements of the AMMs. Therefore, the decision problem of the trader is tied to not only the question of selling or buying a certain share of stock but also to the quantity. To determine the number of shares of stock to trade, we assume that the risk neutral trader tries to maximize its utility (Gjerstad and Dickhaut, 1998) for a stock $i \in \{1,2\}$ in a particular trade t:

(13) $$U(E(V_{i,t}), \text{Costs}_{i,t}^{AMM}(q_{i,t}^{current})) = U(W_{i,t}, \text{Costs}_{i,t}^{AMM}(q_{i,t}^{current})) \to \max!_{\{q_{i,t}^{current}\}}.$$

The utility depends on two factors: the expected value of a share of stock i at time t, $E(V_{i,t})$, which a myopic trader subjectively believes to be $W_{i,t}$ (equation (12)), and the total costs of the shares, $\text{Costs}_{i,t}$, for a trade of $q_{i,t}^{current}$ shares. This number, $q_{i,t}^{current}$, must be optimized to maximize utility. Detailed descriptions of the utility maximization appear in the Appendix.

To obtain a more realistic setting, we set a maximum amount c_t as a budget constraint that limits the maximum amount a trader can spend (buy order) or redeem (sell order). Moreover, for DPA and bHSX, the budget constraint imposes a necessary bound on the number of tradable shares, beyond the parameter of the maximum number of tradable shares. Without this bound, according to equation (1) in the Appendix, traders would always trade the maximum allowable number of shares. Consequently, for a buy order, the total cost must be below c_t, and the total redemption value of a sell order must be below c_t:

(14) $$\left| \text{Costs}_{i,t}^{AMM}(q^{current}) \right| \le c_t.$$

3.3. Overview and Optimization Criterion

The goal of the simulation study is to analyze the AMMs according to the three criteria that we discussed in the introduction, namely, the highest forecasting accuracy with optimal parameters, robustness against parameter misspecifications and noisy trading, and the speed of information incorporation.

As the basis of our evaluations and the parameter optimization, we consider the (implied for DPM) price efficiency, or the degree to which market prices reflect the shares of stocks' true underlying values. We measure price efficiency as the mean absolute error (MAE) over all trading periods, which equals the absolute difference between the market prediction $pred_{1,T,r}$ and the true value $V_{1,t,r}$:

$$(15) \qquad MAE_r = \frac{1}{T} \sum_{t \in \{1,\ldots,T\}} \left| pred_{1,t,r} - V_{1,t,r} \right|,$$

where $pred_{i,t,r}$ is the prediction about the true value of shares of the *i*th stock at time *t* and in the *r*th replication, and $V_{1,t,r}$ is the true value of the shares of the *i*th stock at time *t* and for the *r*th replication. By using all periods, we capture the complete AMM behavior and quality of the predictions, rather than focusing on a single point in time. Using the predictions and the true values of the shares of the first stock to measure the error is essentially the same as using the predictions and true values of the shares of the second stock, because

$$\left(pred_{1,t} - V_{1,t,r} \right)^2 = \left((1 - pred_{2,t,r}) - (1 - V_{2,t,r}) \right)^2 = \left(pred_{2,t,r} - V_{2,t,r} \right)^2.$$

However, because the final prediction may play a role in cases in which the true value does not change, we also report the error obtained after the last trade, or the final absolute error (FAE), for the first criterion when the true value does not change:

$$(16) \qquad FAE_r = \left| pred_{1,T,r} - V_{1,T,r} \right|.$$

3.4. Selection of AMM Parameters

As we outlined in our description of the AMMs, each AMM must be parameterized individually. The focal parameters are the liquidity parameters, which indicate how fast prices react to trading actions. For LMSR (subsidy), DPM (seed money), and DPA (gamma), a higher liquidity parameter means a slower movement of prices, whereas for bHSX, setting the alpha higher signifies a faster movement. The liquidity parameters can be optimized or varied; we provide an overview in Table 2.

Although LMSR and DPM need only one set parameter, DPA and bHSX also must fix at least two more parameters. Both must set a window length that considers the last trading actions (memory parameter). Because an analysis of two or more parameters increases the complexity excessively, we take a window length of 10 as our base value (see Van Bruggen et al., (2008) for both AMMs. Moreover, we test half and twice the window length for comparison, so our windows consist of 5, 10, and 20 periods.

A third parameter (restriction parameter) applies to DPA and bHSX and involves the maximum number of tradable shares. Again, we follow Van Bruggen et al. (2008) and restrict the maximum number to 50 shares per stock. This restriction applies to each trade of the DPA and the total number of trades in the window of the bHSX. The rationale behind this selection states that only a certain number of shares should influence the movement of prices, accomplished in a single trade in the case of DPA but over the whole window for bHSX.

We set all AMMs initially to have share prices of \$0.50 (LMSR, DPA, bHSX) or an implied probability of 50% (DPM).

	LMSR	DPM	DPA	bHSX
1st (liquidity) parameter Values	Subsidy To be optimized	Seed money To be optimized	Gamma To be optimized	Alpha To be optimized
2nd (memory) parameter Values	-	-	Length window 5, 10, 20	Length window 5, 10, 20
3rd (restriction) parameter Values	-	-	Max. # shares per trade Fixed at 50	Max. # shares in window Fixed at 50

Table 2: AMM parameter selection in simulation study

3.5. Market Environment

We create a market environment in which the true values of the shares of stock, signals of traders, type of transaction, and maximum amount to spend or redeem are set for each period. In a study of Google, Cowgill and colleagues (2008) report 70,706 trades in 270 markets, averaging about 262 trades per market. Thus, rounded numbers of 300 trades seem realistic in corporate settings. In this number of periods, shares of either of the two stocks can be traded.

To set the true value, we consider three situations common in PMs. Typically, a PM operator must set the AMM parameters without knowledge of the true underlying value. However, an operator also should know about the potential volatility at which the true value changes, so we assume no, low, and high true value volatility situations. In the first case, the true value is constant over all trading periods and does not experience any volatility. Moreover, we assume in this case that the true value is uniformly distributed over the whole range between 0 and 1, determined once per replication. In the second situation, there is low volatility in the true value, modeled by incorporating a jump in the true value from 0.5 to 0.5 + d, where d is normally distributed with mean 0 and a standard deviation of 0.1. The jump occurs in period 101. The third situation is analogous to the second one, but the standard deviation of the jump is 0.25 instead of 0.1, which implies greater volatility in the true value and a larger expected jump. A PM operator typically faces the same problem and knows that large/small events might happen, for which the AMM parameters must be set.

We outline the remaining specifications, such as the proportion of noisy traders and degree of noise, and offer a complete overview in the Appendix.

4. Results

4.1. Forecasting accuracy

Table 3 provides the results from the parameter optimization for every AMM and volatility case, as well as aggregated results. Averaged over all 6,000 cases, DPM performs best with a MAE of 1.10, and LMSR is slightly worse with a MAE of 1.25. The DPA results in more than twice the error with a MAE of 2.25. The worst performer, bHSX, attains an error of 3.23.

For the no volatility case, the optimal subsidy parameter is 16, which returns a MAE of 1.62. The DPM in this case delivers slightly better results (MAE 1.62), obtained with seed money of 80. However, DPA and bHSX perform substantially worse. The best DPA result occurs with a window length of 5 and gamma of 93 (MAE 3.71). The results barely vary with respect to the length of the window though. We can infer that the DPA with a window length of 10 or 20 has a higher error of only 0.02 and 0.05, respectively. Thus, with regard to window length, the DPA seems be robust. Again, bHSX delivers the worst results, and a window length of 5 is the optimal solution, with a liquidity parameter value alpha of 0.00145 (MAE 4.53). In contrast with DPA, bHSX is very sensitive to the length of the window: With window lengths of 10 and 20, the MAE becomes 5.63 and 7.34, respectively.

In the case of low volatility, the differences among the AMMs are less pronounced. The LMSR achieves a MAE of 0.72, and the DPM again offers a lower MAE of 0.66. In contrast with the no volatility case, the DPA performs only 0.16 points worse (0.82) than the DPM with window lengths of 5 and 10. Again, the bHSX performs worst (MAE 1.27); however, this level, compared with the no volatility case, is a clear improvement.

Finally, in the high volatility case, the results remain similar to those in the previous two cases. Because the last prediction might also be of particular interest, we display these results in Table 3 as well. The mean FAE across all cases is lower for the DPM (0.64) than for the LMSR (0.95). The bHSX once again performs worst (mean FAE 1.82), though the span with the DPA has reduced (mean FAE 1.40).

	LMSR	DPM	DPA					bHSX		
Liquidity par. optimized	Subsidy	Seed money	Gamma (γ)					Alpha (α)		
Length window	n/a	n/a	5		10		20		5	10	20
Max. # shares tradable	n/a	n/a	50		50		50		50	50	50
All volatility cases											
Mean / Median AE	**1.25** / 1.08	**1.10** / 0.99	**2.25** / 1.20		2.28 / 1.20		2.31 / 1.22		**3.23** / 2.14	3.94 / 2.85	5.14 / 3.89
Mean / Median FAE	0.95 / 0.31	0.64 / 0.24	1.40 / 0.61		1.43 / 0.58		1.42 / 0.63		1.82 / 1.22	2.38 / 1.74	3.14 / 2.51
No volatility in true value											
Opt. liquidity par. value	*16*	*80*	*93*		*93*		*104*		*0.00145*	*0.00160*	*0.00200*
Mean / Median AE	**1.62** / 1.44	**1.36** / 1.25	**3.71** / 2.96		3.73 / 2.88		3.76 / 2.95		**4.53** / 4.08	5.63 / 4.98	7.34 / 6.46
Mean / Median FAE	1.30 / 0.47	0.87 / 0.33	2.16 / 1.14		2.28 / 1.15		1.98 / 1.02		2.72 / 2.28	3.29 / 2.91	4.40 / 4.15
Low volatility in true value											
Opt. liquidity par. value	*280*	*643*	*117*		*119*		*108*		*0.00063*	*0.00071*	*0.00087*
Mean / Median AE	**0.72** / 0.62	**0.66** / 0.57	0.82 / 0.64		**0.82** / 0.63		0.84 / 0.66		**1.27** / 0.96	1.67 / 1.28	2.40 / 1.88
Mean / Median FAE	0.46 / 0.17	0.34 / 0.13	0.45 / 0.31		0.42 / 0.29		0.49 / 0.35		0.72 / 0.63	0.96 / 0.83	1.47 / 1.24
High volatility in true value											
Opt. liquidity par. Value	*49*	*141*	*88*		*86*		*82*		*0.00125*	*0.00160*	*0.00172*
Mean / Median AE	**1.43** / 1.18	**1.28** / 1.15	**2.24** / 1.60		2.28 / 1.60		2.34 / 1.65		**3.24** / 2.55	4.31 / 3.42	5.86 / 4.51
Mean / Median FAE	1.09 / 0.19	0.71 / 0.24	1.58 / 0.78		1.60 / 0.79		1.80 / 0.86		2.04 / 1.61	2.88 / 2.53	3.56 / 3.23

Table 3: Optimal parameter values and forecasting accuracy across volatility cases

4.2. Robustness Tests

4.2.1 Robustness against parameter misspecification

We deviate the parameters -75%, -50%, -25%, 25%, 50%, 75%, and 100% from their optimal value and compute the resulting MAEs. In Figure 3, we depict the aggregated results across all volatility cases in relative terms. The results for each of the volatility cases are consistent with those in the aggregated form.

The LMSR and DPM results are least sensitive to the parameter selection on average. We perceive only a weak rise of MAE for both AMMs. Even when we lower the liquidity parameters by 75%, the error increase remains around 20%. A variation in the lower direction has a stronger negative effect on the accuracy than that in the upper direction. For example, when deviating +75% from the optimum, the increases in error are 6.10% and 5.27% for LMSR and DPM, respectively. However when we deviate -75%, the increases are 21.22% and 17.39%. Thus, for those who set market parameters, if they are in doubt about the parameter selection, a higher liquidity parameter that lets prices move more slowly should be preferred.

For the bHSX and especially DPA, the effects of the parameter deviation are stronger. When the bHSX parameter value alpha decreases by 75%, which increases the liquidity, in contrast with the other AMMs, the MAE improves nearly 100%. However, when allowing less liquidity by raising the parameter 75%, the increase of error is less than 20%. Thus, it seems beneficial, when in doubt, to apply higher liquidity parameter values rather than lower ones for the bHSX.

For DPA, gamma liquidity parameter values that are too low have strong consequences for the MAE. The largest increase of error occurs when the deviation is -75% from the optimum, which results in a relative increase of the MAE of more than 500%. Moreover, in relative terms, the DPA is by far the most sensitive AMM, even compared with the bHSX. A small liquidity parameter value results in a larger error than a comparable higher parameter value. For example, if we deviate by ±50%, the resulting increase of MAE is nearly 70% for -50% and slightly over 20% for +50% from the optimum. Thus, more liquidity functions better than less liquidity, similar to the findings for LMSR and DPM.

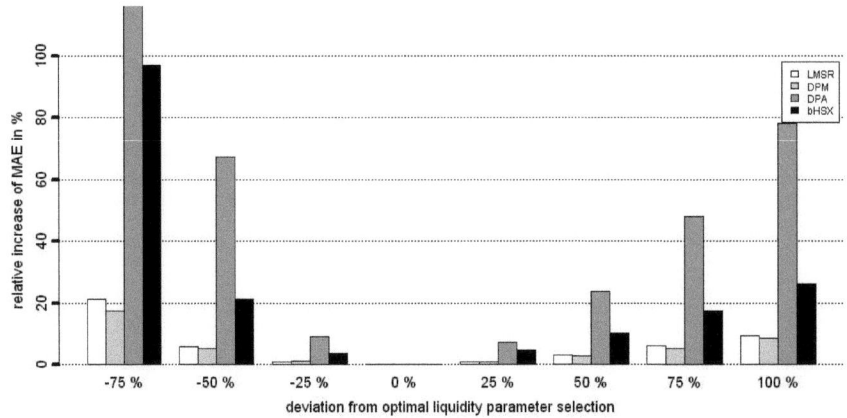

Figure 3: Relative increase of mean absolute errors when deviating from the optimal liquidity parameter value (all volatility cases)

4.2.2 Robustness against noisy trading

We use an analysis of variance (ANOVA) to identify the extent to which the factors for noisy trading—that is, the proportion of noisy traders and the degree of noise—influence the MAE. With a multiple classification analysis (MCA), we also determine how much a factor influences error. We depict the aggregated results over all volatility cases in Table 4: these results are consistent with the single volatility cases.

For both LMSR and DPM, the proportion and degree of noisy traders have significant influences on the MAE ($p < 0.001$). The proportion of noisy traders explains 13.99% and 12.17% of the variance in LMSR and DPM, respectively. The influence of the degree of noise is comparably high, at 16.73% and 11.19%, respectively. In addition, for the LMSR, the MCA shows that a high proportion of noisy traders increases the MAE by 0.279. The degree of noise increases the error by 0.305. For the DPM, results are comparable though not as strong: 0.206 for the proportion and 0.105 for the degree of noise.

The results for the DPA are less clear. The variance explained by the two factors is very low, at 0.30% and 0.22%, respectively, though it remains significant at the 0.1% level for the proportion of noisy traders and at the 0.5% level for the degree of noise. The MCA reveals a value of 0.123 for the proportion and 0.105 for the degree of noisy traders. Thus, both factors influence the MAE, but less strongly than for the LMSR and DPA, especially when it comes to the degree of noise.

	Factor levels for MCA	LMSR		DPM		DPA		bHSX	
		Ex-plained variance	MCA value	Ex-plained variance	MCA value	Ex-plained variance	MCA value	Ex-plained variance	MCA value
All volatility cases									
Average			1.254		1.101		2.253		3.233
Proportion of noisy traders	High	13.99% **	0.279	12.17% **	0.206	0.30% **	0.123	0.00% n.s.	0.011
	Low		-0.279		-0.206		-0.123		-0.011
Degree of noise of noisy traders	High	16.73% **	0.305	11.19% **	0.105	0.22% *	0.105	0.13% n.s.	0.087
	Low		-0.305		-0.105		-0.105		-0.087
% Factors		30.73%		23.36%		0.52%		0.13%	

Table 4: Influence of proportion of noisy traders and degree of noise of noisy traders on MAE aggregated across volatility cases
(*: $p<0.005$, **: $p<0.001$; $N = 6000$ for each AMM)

Finally, for bHSX, the results show that neither the proportion nor the degree of noisy trades have a significant influence ($p > 0.005$) on the MAE. Both factors explain only 0.13% of the variance and reveal MCA values of less than 0.1. Thus, the bHSX is robust against noisy trading on both dimensions.

4.3. Speed of Information Incorporation

Table 5 presents the results that we obtained by measuring the number of periods needed to arrive at a new price level in the case of a jump in the true underlying value. We distinguish the low and high volatility cases (with small and large jumps) that occur during the trading phase.

	LMSR	DPM	DPA	bHSX
Low volatility in true value				
Mean / Median # periods	12.60 / 9	12.44 / 11	21.34 / 21	33.91 / 30
Min / Max / SD # periods	0 / 92 / 14.56	0 / 71 / 10.81	0 / 98 / 13.17	0 / 140 / 22.49
High volatility in true value				
Mean / Median # periods	9.79 / 4	8.13 / 7	18.24 / 18	29.96 / 30
Min / Max / SD # periods	0 / 106 / 17.29	0 / 37 / 6.86	0 / 98 / 12.74	0 / 140 / 22.67

Table 5: Speed of information incorporation

In the low volatility case, LMSR and DPM perform comparably well, and the mean number of periods needed for information incorporation is 12.60 and 12.44, respectively. In contrast, the mean number is approximately 9 periods higher for the DPM (21.34). The bHSX is by far the slowest AMM, with an average of 33.91 periods required to reach the new true value. When the jump is large, as in the case of high volatility, the DPM again performs best: 8.13 periods on average. The margin between it and LMSR also is greater; the latter shows 9.79 periods on average. The DPA performs requires 18.24 periods, followed by the bHSX with almost 30 periods.

5. Conclusion

Choosing an appropriate market mechanism is crucial for forecast accuracy and the success of any prediction market (PM). Many applications show, in practice, that standard continuous double auctions are not well suited for PMs because of their liquidity problems, which implies the need for AMMs. Yet prior literature rarely considers the critical problem of which mechanism to choose.

Our extensive set of simulations reveals that no single best mechanism exists. Rather, each AMM has strengths and weaknesses in different dimensions (Table 6), though LMSR and DPM offer clear advantages in terms of forecast accuracy.

	LMSR	DPM	DPA	bHSX
1. Accuracy	+	++	–	– –
2a. Robustness–parameter selection	++	++	– –	–
2b. Robustness–noisy trading	– –	– –	+/–	++
3. Speed of information incorporation	+	++	–	– –

Table 6: Overview of study results

Regarding the overall highest forecasting accuracy obtained with an optimal parameter selection, LMSR and DPM are superior to both DPA and bHSX. The bHSX returns the worst results overall. When observing the robustness of parameter selection (i.e., deviation of parameters from the optimal selection), we again find that LMSR and DPM perform best.

The liquidity parameter in the case of the DPA is particularly sensitive to deviations, as is window length in the case of bHSX. However, bHSX remains very robust against noisy trading, which occurs when many traders arrive with imperfect information. This property is especially important when many badly informed traders participate in markets or there is a lot of uncertainty about true values. The results pertaining to DPA also show its (slightly lower) robustness to noisy trading. In contrast, both LMSR and DPM are well exposed to noisy trading. With regard to the speed with which new information gets reflected in forecasts, again LMSR and DPM are superior to the other two AMMs. Clearly, robustness against noisy trading and speed of information incorporation represent trade offs.

In conclusion, the LMSR belongs to the group of most versatile AMMs that support many contract designs. Moreover, it delivers good forecasting results in most cases, making it the most complete AMM of all those we have analyzed. The DPM offers some strength in its forecasting results and delivers the best results in three of the four dimensions we measure. However, its major drawbacks pertain to its complex usability for traders, which might prevent less experienced participants from trading, and its limited support of different market designs. With DPA, the only real strength we detect is its offer of a fixed buy and sell price, which can be useful for inexperienced traders. However, the simulations return weak results in most dimensions. Finally, regarding the bHSX, we find poor forecasting accuracy in the simulations. However, we do not use the complete mechanism and have only partial information about this AMM; the actual HSX mechanism uses many more constraints and parameters and therefore likely provide greater accuracy. This improvement also would induce much higher implementation costs to determine those parameters. A major strength of the bHSX, which also should be true for the HSX, is that it barely affected by noisy trading, which might make this mechanism useful in situations with heterogeneous, poorly informed traders.

References

Berg, J., Forsythe, R., Nelson, F. & Rietz, T. (2001) Results from a Dozen Years of Election Futures Markets Research. In Plott, C. & Smith, V. (Eds.) *Handbook of Experimental Economic Results*. Amsterdam, Elsevier.

Chen, K.-Y. & Plott, C. R. (2002) Information Aggregation Mechanisms: Concept, Design and Implementation for a Sales Forecasting Problem. *Working Paper.* California Institute of Technology.

Chen, Y., Pennock, D. M. & Kasturi, T. (2008) An Empirical Study of Dynamic Parimutuel Markets: Evidence from the Tech Buzz Game. *The 10th Workshop on Web Mining and Web Usage Analysis (WebKDD).* Las Vegas.

Cowgill, B., Wolfers, J. & Zitzewitz, E. (2008) Using Prediction Markets to Track Information Flows: Evidence from Google. *Working Paper.* Dartmouth College.

Dahan, E., Soukhoroukova, A. & Spann, M. (2009) New Product Development 2.0: Preference Markets. How Scalable Securities Markets Identify Winning Product Concepts & Attributes. *Journal of Product Innovation Management,* forthcoming.

Das, S. (2005) A Learning Market-Maker in the Glosten-Milgrom Model. *Quantitative Finance,* 5 (2), 169-180.

DeGroot, M. H. & Fienberg, S. E. (1983) The Comparison and Evaluation of Forecasters. *The Statistician,* 32 (1-2), 12-22.

Elberse, A. (2007) The Power of Stars: Do Star Actors Drive the Success of Movies? *Journal of Marketing,* 71 (4), 102-120.

Forsythe, R., Nelson, F., Neumann, G. R. & Wright, J. (1992) Anatomy of an Experimental Political Stock Market. *American Economic Review,* 82 (5), 1142-1161.

Forsythe, R., Rietz, T. A. & Ross, T. W. (1999) Wishes, Expectations and Actions: A Survey on Price Formation in Election Stock Markets. *Journal of Economic Behavior & Organization,* 39 (1), 83-110.

Garman, M. B. (1976) Market Microstructure. *Journal of Financial Economics,* 3 (3), 257-275.

Gjerstad, S. & Dickhaut, J. (1998) Price Formation in Double Auctions. *Games and Economic Behavior,* 22 (1), 1-29.

Glosten, L. R. & Milgrom, P. R. (1985) Bid, Ask and Transaction Prices in a Specialist Market With Heterogeneously Informed Traders. *Journal of Financial Economics,* 14 (1), 71-100.

Hanson, R. (2003) Combinatorial Information Market Design. *Information Systems Frontiers,* 5 (1), 107-119.

Hanson, R. (2007) Logarithmic Market Scoring Rules for Modular Combinatorial Information Aggregation. *Journal of Prediction Markets,* 1 (1), 3-15.

Kehr, C.-H., Krahnen, J. P. & Theissen, E. (2001) The Anatomy of a Call Market. *Journal of Financial Intermediation,* 10 (3-4), 249-270.

Keiser, T. M. & Burns, M. R. (1999) Computer-Implemented Securities Trading System with a Virtual Specialist Function. United States patent number 5,950,176, issued to HSX, Inc.

Keiser, T. M. & Burns, M. R. (2003) Computer-Implemented Securities Trading System with a Virtual Specialist Function. United States 6,505,174 B1, issued to HSX, Inc.

Keiser, T. M. & Burns, M. R. (2006) Computer-Implemented Securities Trading System with a Virtual Specialist Function. United States patent number 7,006,991 B2, issued to CFPH, LL.C.

Kiviat, B. (2004) The End of Management? *TIME, Inside Business.* July 12.

Kleijnen, J. P. C. (1988) Analyzing Simulation Experiments with Common Random Numbers. *Management Science,* 34 (1), 65-74.

Krahnen, J. P. & Weber, M. (2001) Marketmaking in the Laboratory: Does Competition Matter? *Experimental Economics,* 4 (1), 55-85.

Luckner, S. & Weinhardt, C. (2007) How to Pay Traders in Information Markets? Results from a Field Experiment. *Journal of Prediction Markets,* 1 (2), 1-10.

Madhavan, A. (1992) Trading Mechanisms in Securities Markets. *Journal of Finance,* 47 (2), 607-641.

Madhavan, A. (2000) Market Microstructure: A Survey. *Journal of Financial Markets,* 3 (3), 205-258.

Mangold, B., Dooley, M., Flake, G. W., Hoffman, H., Kasturi, T., Pennock, D. M. & Dornfest, R. (2005) The Tech Buzz Game. *Computer,* 38 (7), 94-97.

Nikolova, E. & Sami, R. (2007) A Strategic Model for Information Markets. *Eighth ACM Conference on Electronic Commerce.* San Diego, CA.

O'Carroll, F. M. (1977) Subjective Probabilities and Short-Term Economic Forecasts: An Empirical Investigation. *Applied Statistics,* 26 (3), 269-278.

Pennock, D. M. (2004) A Dynamic Pari-Mutuel Market for Hedging, Wagering, and Information Aggregation. *ACM Conference on Electronic Commerce.* New York.

Pennock, D. M. & Sami, R. (2007) Computational Aspects of Prediction Market. In Nisan, N., Roughgarden, T., Tardos, E. & Vazirani, V. V. (Eds.) *Algorithmic Game Theory.* New York, Cambridge University Press.

Roll, R. (1984) A Simple Implicit Measure of the Effective Bid-Ask Spread in an Efficient Market. *Journal of Finance,* 39 (4), 1127-1139.

Servan-Schreiber, E., Wolfers, J., Pennock, D. M. & Galebach, B. (2004) Prediction Markets: Does Money Matter? *Electronic Markets,* 14 (3), 243-251.

Slamka, C., Soukhoroukova, A. & Spann, M. (2008) Event Studies in Play- and Real Money Prediction Market. *Journal of Prediction Markets,* 2 (2), 53-70.

Snyder, W. W. (1978) Horse Racing: Testing the Efficient Markets Model. *Journal of Finance,* 33 (4), 1109-1118.

Soukhoroukova, A. & Spann, M. (2005) New Product Development with Internet-based Information Markets: Theory and Empirical Application. *13th European Conference on Information Systems.* Regensburg.

Soukhoroukova, A., Spann, M. & Skiera, B. (2009) Creating and Evaluating New Product Ideas with Idea Markets. *Working Paper, University of Passau.*

Spann, M. & Skiera, B. (2003) Internet-Based Virtual Stock Markets for Business Forecasting. *Management Science,* 49 (10), 1310-1326.

Van Bruggen, G. H., Spann, M., Lilien, G. L. & Skiera, B. (2008) Institutional Forecasting: The Performance of Thin Virtual Stock Markets. *Working Paper, Erasmus University.*

Winkler, R. L. (1969) Scoring Rules and the Evaluation of Probability Assessors. *Journal of the American Statistical Association,* 64 (327), 1073-1078.

Wolfers, J. & Zitzewitz, E. (2004) Prediction Markets. *Journal of Economic Perspectives,* 18 (2), 107-126.

Wolfers, J. & Zitzewitz, E. (2008) Interpreting Prediction Market Prices as Probabilities. *NBER Working Paper #12200.* University of Pennsylvania.

Appendix

Examples for Trading Actions

As in the simulations implemented herein, we assume a winner takes all market with two stocks, such that one stock describes an event (e.g., a Democrat becomes President), and the second stock describes a complementary event (e.g., a Republican becomes President). Share prices then reflect (implied) probabilities of the events to happen. All AMMs, if needed, begin with a prediction of 50% for both stock 1 and 2. The trading actions are "Buy 1 share of stock 1," "Buy 3 shares of stock 1," or "Sell 2 shares of stock 2." Moreover, because in general, share prices of both stocks do not equal 1 in DPA and bHSX, we normalize both share prices after every price change to ensure that they do. In the case of the DPA, the shares of stock that have not been traded are adjusted by setting their prices to 1, minus the traded shares of stock. For bHSX, because the shares of both stocks can be traded, we normalize their prices by using their relative prices after the so called "sweep phase," as we show in Table A1.

Logarithmic Market Scoring Rules (LMSR)

The LMSR's only parameter, subsidy, is initially set to 50. There are no shares of stock in the market. Thus, according to equation (3) in the paper, the initial prices of the (infinitesimal) shares of stock are $p_i(\vec{q_0}) = \dfrac{\exp(q_{i,0}/b)}{\sum_{j \in N} \exp(q_{j,0}/b)} = \dfrac{\exp(0/50)}{\exp(0/50) + \exp(0/50)} = \$0.50$ each.

Because the prices of shares of stock correspond to probabilities, the current probability of each event is 50%. For the first trading action, the costs of buying one share of stock 1, according to equations (1) and (2) in the paper, are

$$Costs_{i,t}^{LMSR}(q_{i,t}^{current}) = C(\vec{q_t}) - C(\vec{q_{t-1}})$$
$$= C(\vec{q_1}) - C(\vec{q_0})$$
$$= C((1,0)) - C((0,0))$$
$$= 50 \cdot \ln(\exp(1/50) + \exp(0/50)) - 50 \cdot \ln(\exp(0/50) + \exp(0/50))$$
$$= \$0.502,$$

with $q_{1,1}^{current} = 1$. After the trade, there is one share of stock 1 on the market, and no shares of stock 2. According to equation (3) in the paper, the new price for the share and thus the probability that the event underlying stock 1 will happen is

$p_1(\vec{q_1}) = \dfrac{\exp(1/50)}{\exp(1/50)+\exp(0/50)} = \$0.505 \triangleq 50.5\%$. Accordingly, the new price for stock 2 is $p_2(\vec{q_1}) = \dfrac{\exp(0/50)}{\exp(0/50)+\exp(1/50)} = \$0.495 = \$1 - p_1(\vec{q_1}) = \$1 - \$0.505$. The next trade, "Buy 3 shares of stock 1," then can be computed, with costs of $Costs_{1,2}^{LMSR}(3) = C((4,0)) - C((1,0)) = \$1.537$, which drive the prediction of stock 1's underlying event happening to $p_1(\vec{q_2}) = \dfrac{\exp(4/50)}{\exp(4/50)+\exp(0/50)} = \$0.520 \triangleq 52\%$. In the next step, two shares of stock 2 sell at costs of $Costs_{2,3}^{LMSR}(-2) = C((4,-2)) - C((4,0)) = -\$0.950$, which are negative. Thus, the trader receives $0.95 instead of having to pay for the shares in the case of a purchase. The new and final price of stock 1 is $p_1(\vec{q_3}) = \dfrac{\exp(4/50)}{\exp(4/50)+\exp(-2/50)} = \$0.530$, and event 1 (2) happens with a probability of 53% (47%). If the underlying event occurs, the shares' payoffs are $1; otherwise, they are $0.

Dynamic Pari-Mutuel Market (DPM)

The market begins with 100 shares per stock, which, according to equation (5) in the paper, corresponds to $C(\vec{q_0}) = M^{ini} = \sqrt{\sum_{i \in N} q_{i,0}^2} = \sqrt{100^2 + 100^2} = \$141.421$, the seed money invested in the market. With 100 shares each, according to equation (6) in the paper, the current price for a share of stock 1 or 2 is $p_i(\vec{q_0}) = \dfrac{q_{i,0}}{\sqrt{\sum_{j \in N} q_{j,0}^2}} = \dfrac{100}{\sqrt{100^2 + 100^2}} = \$0.707$. However, because share prices do not correspond to probabilities but must be transformed, the current probability that the event underlying stock 1 or 2 will happen, according to equation (4) in the paper, is $\pi_i(\vec{q_t}) = \dfrac{q_{i,t}^2}{\sum_{j \in N} q_{j,t}^2} = \dfrac{100^2}{100^2 + 100^2} = 0.5 = 50\%$. Buying and selling is similar to the LMSR. Buying one share costs, according to equations (1) and (5) in the paper.

$$Costs_{i,t}^{DPM}(q_{i,t}^{current}) = C(\vec{q_t}) - C(\vec{q_{t-1}})$$
$$= C(\vec{q_1}) - C(\vec{q_0})$$
$$= C((101,100)) - C((100,100))$$
$$= \sqrt{101^2 + 100^2} - \sqrt{100^2 + 100^2}$$
$$= \$0.709.$$

The new probability of the event is $\pi_i(\vec{q_2}) = \dfrac{q_{i,2}^2}{\sum_{j \in N} q_{j,2}^2} = \dfrac{101^2}{101^2 + 100^2} = 50.5\%$, and the remaining calculations work accordingly. The payoff, in contrast to that of the other AMMs, is not \$1 or \$0 but instead depends on the amount of money invested in the market. The total money in the market is, according to equation (5) in the paper, $C(\vec{q_t}) = \sqrt{\sum_{j \in N} q_{j,t}^2} = \sqrt{104^2 + 98^2} = \$142.9$. If event 1 occurs, with 104 shares of the corresponding stock on the market, the money gets split among all shares of stock 1, and the payoff is $\dfrac{M^{final}}{q_{i,T}} = \dfrac{\$142.9}{104} = \$1.37$, but \$0 for all shares of stock 2. If event 2 occurs, all shares of stock 2 are valued at $\dfrac{\$142.9}{98} = \$1.46$.

Dynamic Price Adjustment (DPA)

In contrast to the LMSR, for DPA, we must initialize each stock explicitly with a price for a share of stock, or \$0.5. The liquidity parameter gamma is set to 15, and the length of the moving average window is set to 3. Because the prices are fixed, each share can be bought or sold at a predetermined price: \$0.5 for one share of stocks 1 or 2, and $Costs_{i,t}^{DPA}(q_{i,t}^{current}) = q_{i,t}^{current} \cdot p_{i,t-1} = 1 \cdot \$0.5 = \$0.5$. After the trade, the prices are adjusted according to equation (9) in the paper:

$$p_{i,t}\left(p_{i,t-1}, \overrightarrow{q_{i,t}^{lag}}\right) = p_{i,t-1} + sig\left(q_{i,t,0}^{lag}\right) \cdot \left|q_{i,t,0}^{lag}\right| \cdot \dfrac{p_{i,\max}^2}{\gamma^2} \cdot \dfrac{\sum_{k=0}^{I_t} \left|q_{i,t,k}^{lag}\right|}{I_t + 1} =$$

$$= \$0.5 + \$1 \cdot |1| \cdot \dfrac{1^2}{15^2} \cdot \dfrac{0 + |1|}{1+1} = \$0.502 = p_{1,1}.$$

Now the prices for the shares of the second stock can be adjusted, $p_{2,1} = \$1 - p_{1,1} = \$1 - \$0.502 = \$0.498$, which corresponds to probabilities of 50.2% and 49.8% for event 1 and event 2. In the second trading action, a trader can buy 3 shares of stock 1 for the new fixed price of $Costs_{1,2}^{DPA}(3) = 3 \cdot \$0.502 = \$1.506$. Thereafter, the price of shares of stock 1 adjusts again to $p_{1,2} = \$0.502 + \$1 \cdot |3| \cdot \dfrac{1}{15^2} \cdot \dfrac{|1| + |3|}{3} = \$0.52$, and share prices of stock 2 also adjust. For the last trade, two shares of stock 2 sell for $0.48 each: $Costs_{2,3}^{DPA}(-2) = (-2) \cdot \$0.48 = -\$0.96$. The price is then adjusted, such that $p_{2,3} = \$0.48 - \$1 \cdot |-2| \cdot \frac{1}{15^2} \cdot \frac{|2|}{4} = \$0.476 = \$1 - \$0.524 = \$1 - p_{1,3}$, which drives the last predictions to 52.4% and 47.6%, respectively. The shares' payoffs are either $1 or $0, depending on which event occurs.

Basic Hollywood Stock Exchange (bHSX)

Similar to the DPA, share prices are initialized to $0.5, and the liquidity parameter alpha is set to 0.01. During the sweep phase, orders get accumulated but not executed. Therefore, the bHSX receives two buy orders for $1+3=4$ shares of stock 1 and one sell order of 2 shares of stock 2. During this phase, the final price at which the shares are traded is not known to the traders. At the end of the sweep phase, which has a length of 3 periods, the final trading price can be determined (equation (10) in the paper):

$$p_{i,s}\left(p_{j,s-1}, \overrightarrow{q_{i,s-1}^{sweep}}\right) = p_{i,s-1} + \alpha \cdot \sum_{z=1}^{\left|\overrightarrow{q_{i,s-1}^{sweep}}\right|} q_{i,s-1,z}^{sweep} =$$
$$= \$0.5 + \$0.01 \cdot (1+3) = \$0.54 = p_{1,1}$$

for the shares of the first stock. For the shares of the second stock, the calculations are $p_{2,1} = \$0.5 + \$0.01 \cdot (-2) = \$0.48$. Because the prices of the two shares must sum to 1, we normalize their share prices, such that

$$p_{1,1}^{final} = \frac{p_{1,1}}{p_{1,1} + p_{2,1}} = \frac{\$0.54}{\$0.54 + \$0.48} = \$0.529 = 1 - \$0.471 = \$1 - p_{2,1}^{final}.$$ Thus, the final execution price for buying and selling shares in this sweep phase is $0.529 for a share of stock 1 and $0.471 for a share of stock 2, which implies final predictions of 52.9% and 47.1%, respectively. The costs for the first trade are

$Costs_{i,t}^{bHSX}\left(q_{i,t}^{current}\right) = q_{i,t}^{current} \cdot p_{i,s} = 1 \cdot \$0.529 = \$0.529$, those for the second trade are

$Costs_{1,2}^{bHSX}(3) = 3 \cdot \$0.529 = \$1.587$, and those for the third trade are

$Costs_{2,3}^{bHSX}(-2) = (-2) \cdot \$0.471 = -\$0.942$. The payoffs are the same as those for LMSR and DPA.

		LMSR		DPM		DPA		bHSX	
Set up	Liquidity parameter	subsidy		seed $		gamma		alpha	
	Liquidity parameter value	50		141.4		15		0.01	
	Length window	n/a		n/a		3		3	
		Stock 1	Stock 2	Stock 1	Stock 2	Stock 1	Stock 2	Stock 1	Stock 2
Status before trading	# shares on market	0	0	100	100	0	0	0	0
	Price of share	$0.500	$0.500	$0.707	$0.707	$0.500	$0.500	$0.500	$0.500
	Probability of event (%)	50.0	50.0	50.0	50.0	50.0	50.0	50.0	50.0
1. "Buy 1 share of stock 1"	Costs for trade	$0.502		$0.709		$0.500		n/a yet	
	New # shares on market	1	0	101	100	1	0	1	0
	New price of share	$0.505	$0.495	$0.711	$0.704	$0.502	$0.498	$0.500	$0.500
	New probability of event (%)	50.5	49.5	50.5	49.5	50.2	49.8	50.0	50.0
2. "Buy 3 shares of stock 1"	Costs for trade	$1.537		$2.147		$1.506		n/a yet	
	New # shares on market	4	0	104	100	4	0	4	0
	New price of share	$0.520	$0.480	$0.721	$0.693	$0.520	$0.480	$0.500	$0.500
	New probability of event (%)	52.0	48.0	52.0	48.0	52.0	48.0	50.0	50.0
3. "Sell 2 shares of stock 2"	Costs for trade		$0.950	104	$1.379		-$0.960	n/a yet	
	New # shares on market	4	-2	104	98	4	-2	4	-2
	New price of share	$0.530	$0.470	$0.728	$0.686	$0.524	$0.476	$0.500	$0.500
	New probability of event (%)	53.0	47.0	53.0	47.0	52.4	47.6	50.0	50.0
Calculations for bHSX after sweep phase	Sum of ordered shares in window							4	-2
	Preliminary net price movement							$0.040	-$0.020
	Preliminary new price							$0.540	$0.480
	Norm. price for ordered shares							$0.529	$0.471
	New probability of event							52.9	47.1
	Costs for 1. trade (1 share of stock 1)							$0.529	
	Costs for 2. trade (3 shares of stock 1)							$1.587	
	Costs for 3. trade (-2 shares of stock 2)								-$0.942
Payoff of each share of stock	If event 1 occurs	$1.00	$0.00	$1.37	$0.00	$1.00	$0.00	$1.00	$0.00
	If event 2 occurs	$0.00	$1.00	$0.00	$1.46	$0.00	$1.00	$0.00	$1.00

Table A1: Example of three simple trading actions and resulting payoffs

Determination of Utility Maximizing Number of Traded Shares

For LMSR, DPA, and bHSX, the share prices directly correspond to probabilities and expected values. In the case of LMSR, we can easily observe that utility becomes maximized when the shares are ordered up to the point that the price of the $q_{i,t}^{current}$ th share ordered is less than the valuation $W_{i,t}$ but the price of the $(q_{i,t}^{current}+1)$st share is greater than that valuation. We present these considerations for a buy order, but they are applicable to sell orders as well:

(1)
$$U(E(V_{i,t}), \text{Costs}_{i,t}^{\{LMSR,DPA,HSX\}}(q_{i,t}^{current})) = U(W_{i,t}, \text{Costs}_{i,t}^{\{LMSR,DPA,HSX\}}(q_{i,t}^{current}))$$
$$= \sum_{s=1}^{q_{i,t}^{current}} \left(W_{i,t} - p_{i,t}^{\{LMSR,DPA,HSX\}}(s)\right)$$
$$\rightarrow \max_{\{q_{i,t}^{current}\}}$$
$$\Leftrightarrow$$
$$\begin{bmatrix} p_{i,t}^{LMSR}(q_{i,t}^{current}) \leq W_{i,t} \wedge p_{i,t}^{LMSR}(q_{i,t}^{current}+1) > W_{i,t} \text{, if LMSR} \\ \max\{q_{i,t}^{current}\} \text{, if DPA or HSX} \end{bmatrix}.$$

For the LMSR, the function $p_{i,t}^{LMSR}(\cdot)$ is increasing, because a continuous price function for the pricing of the shares exists. However, for the DPA, the function $p_{i,t}^{DPA}(\cdot)$, and thus the price of each share, is constant. For the bHSX, the rationale is similar, because traders cannot infer the final (constant) price and must assume that the last price is the price they will have to pay.

Prices do not correspond directly to probabilities in the DPM, and expected payoff values must be considered, as analyzed by Nikolova and Sami (2007, lemma 5), who show that a risk neutral trader maximizes surplus when trading with the DPM (for a purchase and the first stock):

(2)
$$U(E(V_{i,t}), \text{Costs}_{i,t}^{DPM}(q_{i,t}^{current})) \rightarrow \max_{\{q^{current}\}}$$
$$\Leftrightarrow$$
$$\frac{q_{1,t}+q_{i,t}^{current}}{q_{2,t}} \leq \sqrt{\frac{\pi_1\left(\vec{q_t}+\left(q_{i,t}^{current},0\right)\right)}{\pi_2\left(\vec{q_t}\right)}} \wedge \frac{q_{1,t}+q_{i,t}^{current}+1}{q_{2,t}} > \sqrt{\frac{\pi_1\left(\vec{q_t}+\left(q_{i,t}^{current}+1,0\right)\right)}{\pi_2\left(\vec{q_t}\right)}}.$$

Detailed Setup of Market Environment

To test the mechanisms' robustness against noisy trading, we analyze the effects of two dimensions: the proportion of noisy traders and the degree of noise when a trader receives a noisy signal. We assume low and high levels of the proportion of noisy traders in the trading crowd. At the low level, there are twice as many informed traders as there are noisy traders; at the high level, the situation is reversed. For the degree of noise, we use a distribution of deviation from the true value of $\sim N(0,0.05)$, as in Das (2005). We leave this setting as our high level and specify the low level as $\sim N(0,0.02)$.

The budget constraint c_t (equation (14) in the paper) is drawn from a normal distribution. We set the mean of the distribution to $5, which is sufficiently high not to have an effect at different levels of share prices on the trading outcome. For a small deviation from $5, we leave the standard deviation rather low at $1. The type of transaction, buy or sell, must be specified for all periods, so we also randomly draw this type. Because the DPM is sensitive to the amount of money in the market, we simulate increasing numbers of traders by setting the probability of a purchase to Pr(Type = 1 = purchase) = 0.6 versus Pr(Type = 0 = sale) = 0.4. Thus, this type is Bernoulli distributed, such that Type $\sim$ Ber(0.6).

For the first criterion, we optimize one (liquidity) parameter for LMSR and DPM. However, we have three window lengths in the case of the DPA and bHSX (5, 10, and 20 periods), so we also must optimize the liquidity parameters individually for each window length. In Table A2, we display only the optimal liquidity parameters. The (much larger) number of parameter combinations required to arrive at this optimal point is omitted for simplicity. We also use the optimal liquidity parameters (for all AMMs) and optimal liquidity parameter/length of window combination to deviate from these values, which reveals 7 cases for each AMM and 28 total cases. The data come from the first criterion. To reduce variance and decrease the number of replications, we use common random numbers (Kleijnen, 1988) for each factor. We set the number of replications to 500, which allows for a wide range of possible trading situations. Thus, we obtain a total of $3 \times 2 \times 2 \times 36 \times 6000 =$ 216,000 observations.

With regard to the first criterion, we obtain three optimal parameters (parameter combinations for DPA/bHSX) per AMM for each volatility case, because we optimize the parameters for three different volatility cases. The global optimum is a function of the liquidity parameter, and the resulting MAE is convex. Too much liquidity moves prices too slowly and increases the error, whereas insufficient low liquidity moves prices too fast, which also increases the error. We conduct the parameter optimization by choosing a very low minimum and very high maximum liquidity value, then use nested intervals to obtain the optimal solution.

Factor	# Levels	Levels	Specifications
Number of trading periods	1	Fixed	300
Expected volatility in true value	3	None	True value constant and $\sim U(0,1)$
		Low	True value jumps in period 101 from 0.5 to $0.5 + d \sim N(0,0.1)$
		High	True value jumps in period 101 from 0.5 to $0.5 + d \sim N(0,0.25)$
Proportion of noisy traders	2	Low	Noisy to informed traders: 1:2
		High	Noisy to informed traders: 2:1
Degree of noise of noisy traders	2	Low	Deviation of noisy traders from true value $\sim N(0,0.02)$
		High	Deviation of noisy traders from true value $\sim N(0,0.05)$
Max. amount to spend/redeem	1	Fixed	$\sim N(\$5, \$1)$
Type of transaction	1	Fixed	Type $\sim Ber(0.6)$
Criterion	36		1. Optimal parameters for minimal error - 1 for LMSR - 1 for DPM - 3 for DPA (lengths window) - 3 for bHSX (lengths window) 2.1. Deviation from optimal parameters - 28 (7 deviations per AMM) 2.2. Noisy trading - 0 (data from criterion 1) 3. Speed of information incorporation - 0 (data from criterion 1)
Number of cases		$3 \times 2 \times 2 \times 36 =$ 432	
Replications per case		500	
Total number of observations		$432 \times 500 =$ 216,000	

Table A2: Design of simulation study

The Price of Running Liquid Prediction Markets

Christian Slamka[1]

[1] School of Business and Economics, Goethe-University Frankfurt

Abstract

Prediction markets have widely emerged, especially in corporate settings. In order to overcome the perpetual problem of illiquidity, many prediction markets apply so called automated market makers as market mechanism for trading. However, because they usually need a subsidy to work, they only have been used in play-money markets, where no real money is at stake and losses for operators cannot occur. In this paper, we analyze the only two automated market makers with upper bounded losses and study the maximum and expected losses. For PM operators, these amounts to subsidize markets can potentially be compared against the costs of running pure play-money markets. Moreover, due to the rather low level of required subsidies, automated market makers seem to be a realistic alternative to traditional market mechanisms in real-money markets.

Keywords: prediction markets, market design, market mechanism, market operations

1. Introduction and Problem

In recent years, interest for prediction markets (PMs) as a promising tool for forecasting has steadily risen. These markets, which started off as a niche application in the field of political forecasting (e.g., Forsythe et al., 1992), have continuously found applications in further areas such as sports forecasting (Servan-Schreiber et al., 2004) and also have continued their way into many company related forecasting fields such as sales forecasting (Chen and Plott, 2002), new product concept evaluation (Dahan et al., 2009, Soukhoroukova and Spann, 2005), or even generation and evaluation of ideas within companies (Soukhoroukova et al., 2009). The reason for their emergence is mainly, besides further advantages such as cost effectiveness and scalability (Dahan et al., 2009), the high forecasting accuracy. Several studies show that PMs, in terms of accuracy, perform mostly superior or at least as good as other, comparable forecasting techniques such as polls (e.g., Berg et al., 2001), official company forecasts (Chen and Plott, 2002), or expert ratings (e.g., Spann and Skiera, 2003).

When designing and running PMs, in general, two very distinct types of PMs can be distinguished: play- and real-money markets (Spann and Skiera, 2003). The former markets use a virtual currency, which does not correspond to any real currency, for trading. Based on the traders' performances in terms of play-money portfolio value, usually prizes are given away to the most successful traders. Consequently, traders have an incentive to perform well, i.e. to input their subjectively best predictions into market forecasts. While these prizes do not necessarily have to be high-valued, or even do not have to exist in some cases (Christiansen, 2007), it is generally believed that some form of incentive to perform well has to be present (Spann and Skiera, 2003), with values ranging up to several thousand Euros (Slamka et al., 2008a). With the latter type, real-money markets, traders invest their own, real money in the markets. As a result, they are incentivized to make profits with the money they have invested (Servan-Schreiber et al., 2004). From a PM operator's perspective, using real money is likely to be preferred from the point of view that he does not have to provide any incentives for participation as he would have to when running play-money markets. Thus, he would save immediate costs for the incentives as well as costs such as handling the incentives[3]. Additionally, more traders might be attracted to these markets,

---

[3] Please note that legal barriers in some countries might restrict the use of real money. This restriction, however, is not discussed in this paper.

generating more trading activity. Furthermore, less knowledgeable traders might be prevented from entering these markets due to aversion to lose money.

At the same time, besides choosing among real or play money, a PM operator must decide on another, crucial question of which underlying market mechanism to use. That is, how to match demand and supply influencing the price of the shares of stock and therewith, predictions. Earlier PMs such as the (real money) Iowa Electronic Markets (Berg et al., 2001) and also most financial exchanges such as the Frankfurt Stock Exchange, employ a standard *continuous double auction (CDA)*, which matches orders of sellers and buyers. Because the CDA does not engage in the transaction itself, which is executed only among market participants, running a CDA is essentially free of financial risk for the operator as he will not suffer any loss. Understandably, this is one of the main reasons why large real-money exchanges, such as *Betfair*, employ it in their trading system.

However, in many small, mainly company internal PMs, the number of traders in markets is very low or the number of stocks per trader is very high (Hanson, 2003). This essentially leads to a "chicken and egg problem": traders are attracted to liquid markets, i.e. markets with a high trading frequency, but on the other hand, liquid markets require many traders (Pennock, 2004). Because of this illiquidity problem, many PMs use so called *automated market makers (AMMs)* as a counterpart for trading. In contrast to the CDA, transactions using AMMs do not occur among market participants, but between the AMM as a piece of software and participants in each buy or sell transaction (Hanson, 2003, Pennock, 2004). By providing instant buy and sell opportunities at transparent prices, participants do not have to wait for matching counteroffers for their offers to be executed. So far, companies such as *Microsoft*, *Yahoo!*, *Inkling*, or the *Hollywood Stock Exchange* are using AMMs for trading in their *play money* exchanges.

In real financial markets, (human) market makers are also employed, e.g. at the NASDAQ (www.nasdaq.com). With respect to funding, human market makers make profits by offering spreads between bid and ask prices (Roll, 1984). The key difference for market makers in financial markets and PMs is that in the latter case, usually after the market closes, the payoff values of the shares are determined depending on the outcome of the underlying event. The AMM has thus to buy back the shares at the payoff values, which might be much higher than it has sold them for.

Consequently, in contrast to CDAs in PMs and market makers in financial markets, a possible loss for operators of AMMs is able to occur. Thus, operators usually have to subsidize the market with a certain amount of money which they will lose in order for the PM to work. While losses do not play a role in play-money markets, they could be harmful when running real-money markets with an AMM. This is most likely the reason no company has started using AMMs with real-money markets yet. Then again, even play-money markets cannot be run for free, as traders have to be incentivized with potentially high prizes to trade in the markets. Consequently, it might even be cheaper to run real-money markets with a subsidized AMM than running play-money markets with giving out prizes. However, it is essential for operators to know in advance with how much money they will have to subsidize the market with at most, and have an upper bound on the loss. So for PM operators, a crucial task is to implement a market mechanism which assures a strict bound on the maximum loss and will not let the loss potentially grow to infinity. While AMMs as described in Van Bruggen et al. (2008) or Keiser and Burns (2006) do not have a bounded loss, only the *market scoring rules* (Hanson, 2003, Hanson, 2007) by Hanson and the *dynamic parimutuel market* by Pennock (Pennock, 2004) have predetermined upper bounds on their loss. Nonetheless, to the best of our knowledge, there has been no evaluation this far on a) what the maximum loss running either AMM are, and, b) what the average loss is in order to achieve good forecasting results. Our objective is to answer these two questions by conducting a simulation study, enriched with data from a real-world, real-money PM. In Section 2, we describe the two focal mechanisms and their functioning. Subsequently, we describe the market model we use for our evaluations. In Section 4, we outline the design of the simulation study, followed by the results we obtained in Section 5. In Section 6, we draw the conclusions.

2. Descriptions of Mechanisms

Both mechanisms we analyze are parameterized with a single parameter each. These parameters both control the maximum amount an operator can lose when running the markets, as well as the liquidity of the markets, i.e. the speed at which the share prices move. The higher the parameter values, the higher the possible maximum loss and the slower the prices move. In order to make this fact clearer, consider a share of stock which is currently valued rather low. Consequently, the AMM offers shares of stock at a low price, and traders buy shares. Now after the close of the market, supposed the shares are valued significantly higher than the AMM has sold them for to traders, the operator loses money as he has to buy back the shares from the traders at this high price, which is the current loss. Now supposed the liquidity parameter value is lower, the prices for shares rise more quickly, i.e. traders have to pay more for a share than they would have to with a high liquidity parameter value. In consequence, this means that the loss is lower in this case as fewer "cheap" shares are sold.

2.1. (Logarithmic) Market Scoring Rules

Market scoring rules (MSRs) build up on the long known concept of *scoring rules*, which have been used to evaluate a forecaster's performance (e.g., Winkler, 1969). By being evaluated with scoring rules, forecasters are incentivized to reveal their subjectively most accurate predictions. With simple scoring rules, forecasters give isolated, one time predictions, such as the prediction if it rains on a specific day in the future. However, the basic, but ground braking idea of Hanson's market scoring rules (Hanson, 2003, Hanson, 2007) is that forecasters give successive predictions on one particular forecasting goal by adjusting the former, most current, prediction and giving the second to last predictor the amount this forecaster has betted. The amount this forecaster receives for his prediction is the *improvement* of prediction. This number, which can be negative, if it turns out the forecaster has moved the prediction in the "wrong" direction, i.e., farther away from the actual outcome than his predecessor has forecasted. The concept of moving estimates can be modeled by introducing shares of underlying events which can be traded, and have a final value of $1, if the particular event happens, and $0, otherwise. With an underlying continuous price function, which is derived from the particular scoring rule being used, the MSR determines the price for each share which is sold or bought. The number of bought shares is positively correlated with the price of shares.

In general, MSRs work with a set of N mutually exclusive and exhaustive outcomes, such that the probabilities of all outcomes sum up to one at any point in time a market is running. While in theory, any proper scoring can be used for market scoring rules, the logarithmic scoring rule $s(p) = b \log(p)$ (Hanson, 2003) has been applied in the wide majority of cases, which include the markets of Inkling or Microsoft's internal markets. The *subsidy b* controls the *maximum* amount of money the AMM can lose as well as the liquidity in the market. Because forecasters pay off the last forecaster before them according to the scoring rule, the operator only has to reimburse the last forecaster for his predictions. Additionally, the very first forecaster has already paid the *initial* amount at the very first trade. Thus, the loss is:

(1) $\quad \text{loss}^{LMSR} = b \cdot \ln p_{last} - b \cdot \ln p_{ini} = b \cdot \ln p_{last} + b \cdot \ln \frac{1}{p_{ini}} \leq b \cdot \ln \frac{1}{p_{ini}} \overset{p_{ini}=1/N}{=} b \cdot \ln N$.

The loss' upper bound of $b \cdot \ln N$ is reached if and only if each share's price is, during market trading, driven to the final payoff[4]. For instance, if traders in the market very strongly believe that an event will happen, they drive the prices of the share very close to 1, implying a prediction of almost 100% that the event will happen. If now the event actually happens, the operator has to pay off the last trader according to the logarithmic scoring rule.

2.2. Dynamic Pari-Mutuel Market

Standard pari-mutuel markets are known from e.g. horse races and are recognized to be able to aggregate information efficiently at one point in time (Snyder, 1978). At any time before the close of the market, money can be spent on each of the N mutually exclusive and exhaustive outcomes, e.g., on the victory of a particular horse. After the close of the market, the total money spent on all possible outcomes is $M = \sum_{j \in N} m_j$, where m_j is the amount betted on outcome j. When the final outcome is known, each Euro invested in the "correct" event i is then worth $\frac{M}{m_i} \€ \geq 1\€$. But pari-mutuel markets are not able to update predictions on the arrival of new information, such as news (Pennock, 2004). However in PMs, an update of prediction as a reaction to news is a crucial feature, as the "value" of an event can be determined (Slamka et al., 2008b). This is because participants in pari-mutuel markets are not incentivized to trade before the close of the market, since regardless of the point in time of the investment, a share of the outcome will be equally expensive if bought long before the close of the market. Consequently, reacting to events before the close of the market cannot be achieved with this mechanism.

---

[4] We make the assumption that with N shares, each share is initialized to the equal price of 1/N.

The dynamic pari-mutuel market (DPM, Pennock, 2004), which is, e.g., applied in the Yahoo! Buzz markets, overcomes this problem by introducing dynamic prices for shares of the final amount of money, rather than having a fixed price as with the standard mechanism. The price of a share depends, similar to the MSRs, on the number of shares in the market and on the utilized price function (Pennock and Sami, 2007). As in the standard pari-mutuel market, all money is redistributed over all winning shares and the price of a share does not directly correspond to actual probabilities, but has to be transformed into probabilities.

When starting the market and in order to allow for trading, an initial amount of $C(\vec{q}^{ini}) = M^{ini}$ and a vector $\vec{q}^{ini}$ of shares containing quantities of each must be assigned[5]. The price function $C(\cdot)$ denotes a 1-to-1 mapping between the vector of shares and the money in the market (Pennock and Sami, 2007). Similarly to the subsidy b seen with MSRs, the initial assignment of money/shares controls the liquidity of the market and maximum loss. At the close of the market, there are $|\vec{q}^{final}|$ shares on the market, with corresponding money $C(\vec{q}^{final})$ totally invested in the shares. Now if the event which occurs out of the N events is i, all the money invested in all shares is equally split among the holders of the share. Thus the value of the share of the occurring event i is $\dfrac{M^{final}}{q_i^{final}}$, where M^{final} denotes the total amount of money invested in all shares, including the seed money, and q_i^{final} is the final number of shares of i in the market. The amount of shares of i the operator holds at the end of the market is $\min\{q_i^{ini}, q_i^{final}\}$ because the maximum number of shares is either the initially assigned number of shares, or, if more shares have been sold than bought, the final number of shares. Consequently, the loss for the operator is

(2) $$\text{loss}^{DPM} = M^{ini} - \min\{q_i^{ini}, q_i^{final}\} \cdot \dfrac{M^{final}}{q_i^{final}} \leq M^{ini},$$

and thus, the upper bound for loss is M^{ini}, which is the amount initially invested.

---

[5] As with the MSR, we assume all N events to be equally likely and, thus, the elements of the initial vector of number of shares are equal.

3. Market Model

As a basis for our simulations, we introduce a microstructure market model uniquely designed for AMMs in PMs which we have obtained by extending a model introduced by Das (Das, 2005), which itself is an extended model of Glosten and Milgrom (Glosten and Milgrom, 1985). The contributed extension of the model (section 3.2) is necessary due to PM and AMM specific properties of the markets, i.e. the existence of two stocks in a market and the varying order quantities as opposed to one stock and a fixed order quantity, respectively.

3.1. Basic Model

In the basic model of Das (2005), one single stock in the market exists which shares can only be traded by intermediation of a market maker, i.e. one transaction side is always the market maker, and the opposite side is always a trader. Traders in the market arrive one by one in discrete points in time $t \in \{1,...,T\}$. The size of a trade is fixed to one unit each trade, in every period the market maker issues bid and ask prices for one unit, $P_{i,t,b}$ and $P_{i,t,a}$ respectively. The share of stock i has an underlying true value of $V_{i,t}$, which is exogenously given. There are two types of risk neutral traders: perfectly informed traders which are exactly aware of the share's true value $V_{i,t}$, and noisy informed traders which receive a noisy signal with mean zero on average. Thus, a single trader receives the following signal of the share's valuation:

(3) $$W_{i,t} = \begin{cases} V_{i,t}, & \text{if trader at time } t \text{ trading } i\text{th stock is perfectly informed,} \\ V_{i,t} + \omega(0, \sigma_{noisy}), & \text{if trader at time } t \text{ trading } i\text{th stock is noisy informed.} \end{cases}$$

In consequence, a traders issues a sell order if $W_{i,t} < P_{i,t,b}$, i.e. he assumes the share to be overvalued or issues a buy order if $W_{i,t} > P_{i,t,a}$ for an (subjectively) undervalued share. If the signal lies within the spread, such that $P_{i,t,b} \leq W_{i,t} \leq P_{i,t,a}$, no order is issued.

3.2. Extension of the Model

In PMs, several market designs exists (Spann and Skiera, 2003), whereas the "winner takes all" market is the most common design and also, is supported by both MSR and DPM. In this market design, at least two stocks exist where in the end, exactly one stock "wins", i.e. the underlying event actually occurs. A classic example would be horse races with, e.g., two stocks of two horses, of which one will win$_2$. This implies that the market model has to be extended to two stocks, which is the simplest form of a multi outcome, winner takes all market. The *true values* $V_{1,t}$ of the share of the first and $V_{2,t}$ of the share of second stock denote the probabilities to win in period t, and are constant in this model. The probabilities of winning, and thus, the true values, always sum up to 1, such that $V_{2,t} = 1 - V_{1,t}$ in every period t. All traders are assumed to be aware of this property, which implies that we can infer that the signal $W_{2,t}$, can be obtained by calculating $W_{2,t} = 1 - W_{1,t}$ (which equal the share prices and thus probabilities in case of MSR and the implied probabilities in case of DPM). The choice of a buy or sell order is given. If a buy order is chosen, the undervalued share (relative to $W_{i,t}$) is traded, if a sell order is chosen, the overvalued share is traded.

The second extension of the model aims at the restriction of the trading quantity to one share per period, which we suspend because different order quantities are essential for the price movements of the AMMs. Due to this relaxation, the decision problem of the trader is not only tied to the question of selling or buying the share of stock, but also to which quantity. In order to determine the number of shares to trade, we assume that the risk neutral trader tries to maximize its expected utility (Gjerstad and Dickhaut, 1998) for a share of stock $i \in \{1,2\}$ in a particular trade. Thus, for the MSR and in case of a purchase, a trader buys shares until the price per share is above the trader's valuation. By doing this, a trader maximizes his expected utility in a trade. As prices do not directly correspond to probabilities in the DPM and expected payoffs also have to be considered, a similar analyses has been made in (Pennock and Sami, 2007, lemma 5), in which the authors show how a risk neutral trader maximizes his surplus when trading with the DPM. Additionally, in order to obtain a more realistic setting, we set a maximum amount c_t as budget constraint to limit the maximum amount a trader can spend (in case of of a buy order) or redeem (in case of a sell order). Thus, (here in case of a buy order), the total cost of a buy order has to be below c_t, while the total redemption value of a sell order is also below c_t.

4. Design of Simulation Study

The general idea of the design of the simulation study is to determine the amount of money which the market has to be subsidized with in order to obtain the best possible forecasting result. As the extent of losses is positively correlated with the liquidity with both AMMs, we try to find the optimal amount of losses which neither provides too much (slow moving (implied) probabilities) nor too low (fast moving (implied) probabilities) liquidity. If we only tried to minimize the amount of money to subsidize the market with, market results would very likely be useless, as little money to subsidize implies very volatile markets which would have no use as a forecasting instrument. So we assume that the top priority for PM operators in the long run is to achieve good forecasting results and thereafter, analyze the losses needed to arrive at these results. By *goodness* of a result we denote the prediction accuracy of the actual outcome at the close of a market, i.e. the last prediction. We use the *root mean squared error* (*RMSE*) over all replications of a certain AMM parameter combination, which is calculated as the root of the mean squared difference of the actual market prediction, namely the probability $prob_{1,T,r}$, and the true value $V_{1,r}$:

$$(4) \qquad RMSE = \sqrt{\frac{1}{\#replications} \sum_{r \in \{1,...,\#replications\}} \left(prob_{1,T,r} - V_{1,r} \right)^2 }.$$

We illustrate the study's parameter selections Table 1. Because we deal with real-money markets, we assume that only perfectly informed as well as noisy informed trading exist, each with equal probability of 0.5 of occurrence (Das, 2005), thus the distribution of informed trading is Bernoulli distributed Ber(0.5). If noisy trading occurs, then the standard deviation from the true value, σ_{noisy}, is 0.05, or 5 percentage points. This value has for instance been used by Das (2005). Now in order to capture the effect of an increasing flow of money into the market, we set the probability of a buy order to occur to 0.6 > 0.5, leaving a chance of 0.4 of a sell order to occur in a trading period. Thus, the occurrence of a buy order is again Bernoulli distributed Ber(0.6). This value could also be observed in experimental runs in university internal tests. We are confident that these parameter selections are robust to deviations as we try to find the optimal AMM parameter values by the *final* error. Thus, deviations in simulation parameter will change the absolute level of error, but not the resulting optimal AMM parameter selection.

Parameter	Distribution	Random values drawn in each
Informed trading	Ber(0.5)	replication and period
Distribution of deviation from true value (noise)	N(0,0.05)	replication and period
Type of transaction	Ber(0.6)	replication and period
Max. amount to buy/redeem from Bluevex data set	U(0,1)	replication and period
Share's constant true value	U(0,1)	replication
Number of periods	100 and 1000	
AMMs	LMSR, DPM	
Replications	1000	
Total number of observations	2 x 2 x1000 = 4000	

Table 1: Simulation study design

For the determination of the maximum amount to spend/redeem per trade, we use actual data from a real-money exchange (*Bluevex*) of the European soccer championships 2004 which used a CDA. Descriptives on the data can be found in (Slamka et al., 2008b). For each game, there is a market with three stocks: "Team 1 wins", "Team 2 wins" or "Draw", each paying 10 € if the event happened. In order to fit the data to our problem, we only consider the shares of the team wins in our data. Also, we divide all pricing data by 10, as the payoff in this study is 1 € rather than 10 €. We select the amount bid in each transaction as one data point, resulting in 74,086 data points for both buy and sell transactions. We randomly choose among the values of each order type, each value being equally likely to be drawn. As we do not set any priors on the true value of a share of stock, we thus assume every true value of the share of the first stock, $V_{1,t}$, to be equally likely in the range of 0 to 1. We set the number of trading periods to 100 and 1000 as displayed. In total, we conduct 1000 replications per AMM / parameter selection case for two different numbers of periods, asserting a plethora of possible market situations, resulting in a total of 4000 observations.

5. Results

As our first goal is to obtain optimal parameter values with respect to the lowest RMSE of the prediction of the last trade, we apply a manual iterative procedure to determine them. We optimize to the point an integer number for the "subsidy" parameter (LMSR) or "seed money" (DPM), respectively, is found.

		LMSR	DPM
100 periods	Optimal parameter	Subsidy = 20 €	Seed money = 25 €
	Obtained RMSE	2.804	2.765
	Theoretical max. loss	*13.86 €*	*25 €*
1000 periods	Optimal parameter	Subsidy = 258 €	Subsidy = 266 €
	Obtained RMSE	2.735	2.634
	Theoretical max. loss	*178.83 €*	*266 €*

Table 2: Optimal parameter values and implications for theoretical maximum losses

As it can be inferred from Table 2, a "subsidy" of 20 € (258 € for 1000 periods) for the LMSR and 25 € (266 €) "seed money" for the DPM, respectively, minimize the RMSE. The error values are slightly, but not significantly ($p>0.1$, paired t-test) lower (0.039 / 0.101 for 100/1000 periods) for the DPM compared to the LMSR. Thus, regarding prediction accuracy, both AMMs do not differ. We can now, according to equations (1) and (2), calculate the theoretical maximum loss, which is 20 € x ln(2) = 13.86 € (258 € x ln(2) = 178.83 €) for the LMSR and the complete seed money of 25 € (266 €) for the DPM. So these are the upper maximum bounds of money a PM operator could lose in theory. Thus, at first sight, the LMSR seems to be superior in terms of maximum possible loss, as 13.86 € << 25 € and 178.83 € << 266 €, respectively.

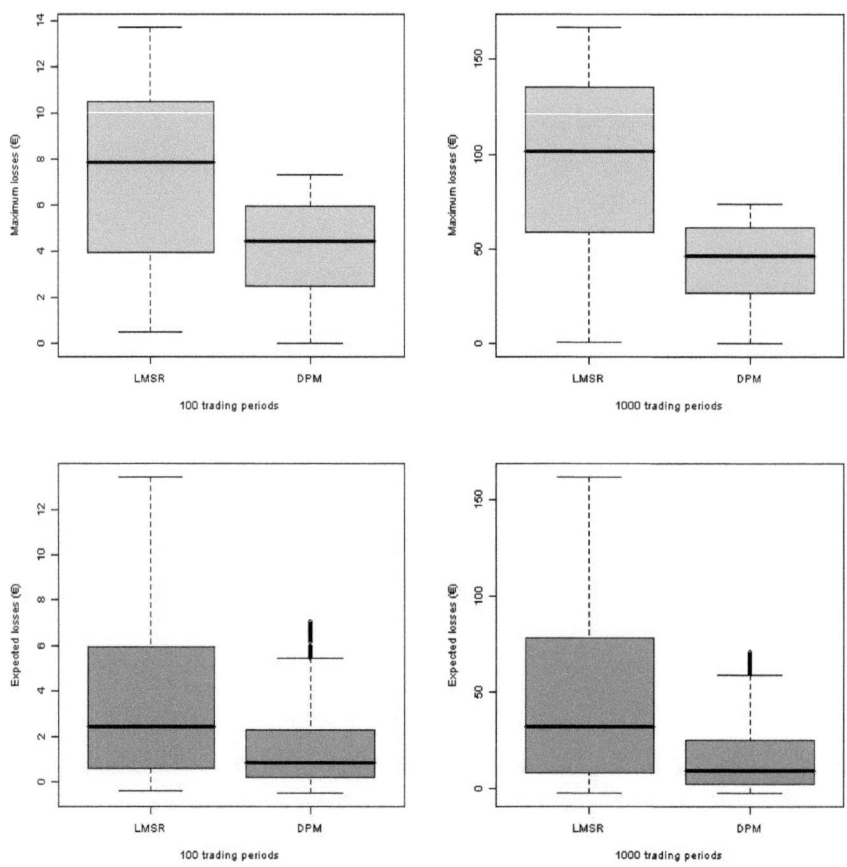

Figure 2: Maximum and expected losses for each AMM

However, although the LMSR has a lower theoretical loss, the upper bounds in equations (1) and (2) might not be equally strict. So in the DPM's bound, the values of the remaining shares which the operator has in its portfolio and which might be valued at a price greater than zero, are not considered. Thus, in order to arrive at a more realistic setting, we analyze both maximum and expected loss which can occur given a final state of the market and possible outcomes (either S_1 or S_2 wins) with respective probabilities as true value of a share. The results are depicted as box plots in Figure 2 and in Table 3. The maximum loss when considering simulation market data are significantly ($p<0.001$) higher for the LMSR with both 100 and 1000 periods. The maximum possible loss which can be encountered is only 7.35 € (73.55 €) with the DPM, as opposed to 13.75 € (€167.22 €) with the LMSR. Notably, the 7.35 € (73.55 €) loss of the DPM of the theoretical loss (see Table 3) is only 29.4 % (27.65 %) of the maximum, implying a very high upper bound on the theoretical loss stated by equation (2). On the other hand, the maximum loss of the LMSR is 99.21 % (93.51 %), and thus, very close to the maximum theoretical loss. In practice, this means that when initializing a PM and precalculating the theoretical loss, with the LMSR the loss can be as high as more than 90 % of the theoretical loss, while with the DPM, a single loss will be no more than roughly 30 % of the theoretical loss (Table 3).

		LMSR	DPM
100 periods	Maximum loss / % of theoretical max. loss	13.75 € *99.21 %*	7.35 € *29.40 %*
	Expected avg. loss / % of theoretical max. loss	3.66 € *26.41 %*	1.50 € *6.00 %*
1000 periods	Maximum loss / % of theoretical max. loss	167.22 € *93.51 %*	73.55 € *27.65 %*
	Expected avg. loss / % of theoretical max. loss	47.06 € *26.32 %*	16.31 € *6.13 %*

Table 3: Absolute and relative maximum and mean expected losses

However, besides the *maximum* loss, a PM operator should also be interested in the *expected* loss, when, e.g., running several markets. The expected loss includes the respective winning probabilities of the shares that can be calculated as follows (for a replication *r*):

(5) $$loss_{exp}^{LMSR/DPM} = V_1 \cdot loss_{S1\_wins}^{LMSR/DPM} + V_2 \cdot loss_{S2\_wins}^{LMSR/DPM}.$$

The expected mean loss for the DPM periods is 1.50 € (16.31 € for 1000 periods), while it is significantly higher with 3.66 € (47.06 €) for the LMSR (lower boxes in Figure 2). According to Table 3, the loss which can be expected is about a quarter of the theoretical loss for the LMSR, while it is under 10 % for the DPM of the maximum theoretical loss.

From Table 3, it can be inferred that the maximum and expected loss are roughly linear with respect to the number of trading periods in both AMM cases. E.g., the average expected loss for the LMSR/DPM is 47.06 €/ 16.31 € compared to 3.61 € / 1.50 €, which are factors of 12.9/10.9 with 10 times the number of trading periods. However, in order to find more support for this statement, future research should more thoroughly vary the number of trading periods in order to obtain more exact results.

6. Conclusion and Discussion

In this paper, we analyze two automated market making mechanisms with bounded loss, which allow for infinite liquidity in markets with few potential traders, which are usually to be found in company internal markets. Both market mechanisms perform indistinguishably well in terms of forecasting accuracy. However, the dynamic pari-mutuel market is superior to the logarithmic scoring rules with respect to the loss which occurs when operating a market. Specifically, when using the DPM, in short markets with only few trades, a mean loss of as low as 1.50 € is sufficient to provide liquidity, whereas the LMSR needs 3.66 € on average. Also, we find initial support that the amount of losses is roughly linear with respect to the number of trading periods.

This amount of money can potentially be compared to the incentives which must be given to participants in order to encourage participation in play-money markets. Thus, depending on the area of application, it might even be less costly to subsidize a real-money market than to provide participants with high incentives. Additionally, because the absolute level of losses needed is rather low, using automated market makers instead of continuous double auctions in real-money markets seems to be a realistic alternative.

Limitations of this study have to be attributed to its simulative nature. Mainly, it is not clear if traders behave equally expected utility maximizing when exposed to different market mechanisms in reality. This might change the trading behavior and thus elicit deviations from the stylized market model. However, this should not have a significant impact on the general conclusions about the level of sustained losses found in this study. One more limitation is also given to the fact that only two stocks are analyzed, and that the results cannot easily be generalized to more stocks. However, in the majority of cases PMs work with simple yes/no questions, which is exactly the model this paper describes.

References

Berg, J., Forsythe, R., Nelson, F. & Rietz, T. (2001) Results from a Dozen Years of Election Futures Markets Research. In Plott, C. & Smith, V. (Eds.) *Handbook of Experimental Economic Results.* Amsterdam, Elsevier.

Chen, K.-Y. & Plott, C. R. (2002) Information Aggregation Mechanisms: Concept, Design and Implementation for a Sales Forecasting Problem. *Working Paper.* California Institute of Technology.

Christiansen, J. D. (2007) Prediction Markets: Practical Experiments in Small Markets and Behaviours Observed. *Journal of Prediction Markets,* 1 (1), 17–41.

Dahan, E., Soukhoroukova, A. & Spann, M. (2009) New Product Development 2.0: Preference Markets. How Scalable Securities Markets Identify Winning Product Concepts & Attributes. *Journal of Product Innovation Management,* forthcoming.

Das, S. (2005) A Learning Market-Maker in the Glosten-Milgrom Model. *Quantitative Finance,* 5 (2), 169-180.

Forsythe, R., Nelson, F., Neumann, G. R. & Wright, J. (1992) Anatomy of an Experimental Political Stock Market. *American Economic Review,* 82 (5), 1142-1161.

Gjerstad, S. & Dickhaut, J. (1998) Price Formation in Double Auctions. *Games and Economic Behavior,* 22 (1), 1-29.

Glosten, L. R. & Milgrom, P. R. (1985) Bid, Ask and Transaction Prices in a Specialist Market With Heterogeneously Informed Traders. *Journal of Financial Economics,* 14 (1), 71-100.

Hanson, R. (2003) Combinatorial Information Market Design. *Information Systems Frontiers,* 5 (1), 107-119.

Hanson, R. (2007) Logarithmic Market Scoring Rules for Modular Combinatorial Information Aggregation. *Journal of Prediction Markets,* 1 (1), 3-15.

Keiser, T. M. & Burns, M. R. (2006) Computer-Implemented Securities Trading System with a Virtual Specialist Function. United States patent number 7,006,991 B2, issued to CFPH, LL.C.

Pennock, D. M. (2004) A Dynamic Pari-Mutuel Market for Hedging, Wagering, and Information Aggregation. *ACM Conference on Electronic Commerce.* New York.

Pennock, D. M. & Sami, R. (2007) Computational Aspects of Prediction Market. In Nisan, N., Roughgarden, T., Tardos, E. & Vazirani, V. V. (Eds.) *Algorithmic Game Theory.* New York, Cambridge University Press.

Roll, R. (1984) A Simple Implicit Measure of the Effective Bid-Ask Spread in an Efficient Market. *Journal of Finance,* 39 (4), 1127-1139.

Servan-Schreiber, E., Wolfers, J., Pennock, D. M. & Galebach, B. (2004) Prediction Markets: Does Money Matter? *Electronic Markets,* 14 (3), 243-251.

Slamka, C., Luckner, S., Seemann, T. & Schröder, J. (2008a) An Empirical Investigation of the Forecast Accuracy of Play-Money Prediction Markets and Professional Betting Markets. *European Conference on Information Systems.* Galway, Ireland.

Slamka, C., Soukhoroukova, A. & Spann, M. (2008b) Event Studies in Play- and Real Money Prediction Market. *Journal of Prediction Markets,* 2 (2), 53-70.

Snyder, W. W. (1978) Horse Racing: Testing the Efficient Markets Model. *The Journal of Finance,* 33 (4), 1109-1118.

Soukhoroukova, A. & Spann, M. (2005) New Product Development with Internet-based Information Markets: Theory and Empirical Application. *13th European Conference on Information Systems (ECIS).* Regensburg.

Soukhoroukova, A., Spann, M. & Skiera, B. (2009) Creating and Evaluating New Product Ideas with Idea Markets. *Working Paper, University of Passau.*

Spann, M. & Skiera, B. (2003) Internet-Based Virtual Stock Markets for Business Forecasting. *Management Science,* 49 (10), 1310-1326.

Van Bruggen, G. H., Spann, M., Lilien, G. L. & Skiera, B. (2008) Institutional Forecasting: The Performance of Thin Virtual Stock Markets *ERIM Report Series.*

Winkler, R. L. (1969) Scoring Rules and the Evaluation of Probability Assessors. *Journal of the American Statistical Association,* 64 (327), 1073-1078.

Second-Generation Prediction Markets for Information Aggregation: A Comparison of Payoff Mechanisms

Christian Slamka[1], Wolfgang Jank[2], Bernd Skiera[1]

[1]School of Business and Economics, Goethe-University Frankfurt
[2]Robert H Smith School of Business, University of Maryland

Abstract

We find that G2 payoff mechanisms perform almost as well as their G1 counterpart, and trading behavior is very similar in both markets (i.e., trading prices and trading volume), except during the very last trading hours of the market. These results indicate that G2 PMs are valid instruments and support their applicability shown in previous studies for developing new product ideas or evaluating new product concepts.

Initial applications of prediction markets (PMs) indicate they provide good forecasting instruments in many settings, such as elections, the box office, or product sales. One particular characteristic of these "first generation" (G1) PMs is that they link the payoff value of a stock's share to the outcome of an event. Recently, "second generation" (G2) PMs have introduced alternative mechanisms to determine payoff values which allow them to be used as preference markets for determining preferences for product concepts or as idea markets for generating and evaluating new product ideas. Three different G2 payoff mechanisms appear in existing literature, but they have never been compared. This study conceptually and empirically compares the forecasting accuracy of the three G2 payoff mechanisms and investigates their influence on participants' trading behavior.

Keywords: prediction markets, preference markets, idea markets, forecasting, decision making, new product development

1. Introduction

Prediction markets (PMs) have emerged as powerful instruments for information aggregation since the late 1980s (Forsythe et al., 1992). Studies in various fields demonstrate their strong forecasting accuracy compared with alternative instruments in politics (Berg et al., 2003, Forsythe et al., 1999), sports (Servan-Schreiber et al., 2004, Spann and Skiera, 2009), and business (Chen and Plott, 2002, Spann and Skiera, 2003, Ortner, 1998). However, these first generation (G1) PMs rely on the outcome of the event to determine the shares of stock's value, that is, the *payoff value*. Because of this limitation, they apply primarily in settings in which the outcome of a stock's underlying event can be known soon after the market closes. This requirement limits their use, especially in internal corporate settings, because many managerial decisions focus on events that may never occur or have a long time horizon. For example, in decisions among alternate product designs, the outcome of the design (i.e., market success or failure) may be known only a long time hence, and managers will never know what might have happened had they implemented different designs. In that sense, G1 PMs cannot determine the payoff value for new product designs, investments, or other managerially relevant questions.

To overcome this shortcoming, recent research proposes second generation (G2) PMs, referred to as *preference markets* by Chan et al. (2002), who, along with Dahan and Hauser (2002), refer to these markets as "Securities Trading of Concepts." That is, they trade concepts of products to forecast expected market shares. Subsequent research has focused on investigating the costs, scalability, and duration of G2 PMs (Dahan et al., 2009, Soukhoroukova and Spann, 2005). Another type of G2 PM pertains to the *idea market*, which is similar to preference markets in that participants trade concepts to evaluate the success of different product or design alternatives. However, in contrast with preference markets, idea markets allow participants to create and introduce their own ideas. In these markets, idea creation and evaluation combine into a single instrument; LaComb et al. (2007) Soukhoroukova et al. (2008) support their use to aid in new product development.

Interest in G2 PMs is rising, not only in academics but also in practice. Several PM companies have shifted from offering purely G1 PMs to providing both preference and idea markets. NewsFutures, for example, a leading PM software provider, now includes preference and idea markets in its standard solution portfolio. Firms such as XPree (which offers "Open Innovation Markets") and Nosco ("Idea Exchange") increasingly are shifting away from offering only PMs to enable short and medium term forecasting and instead are creating and evaluating innovations.

The main difference between G2 and G1 PMs is that in the former, the outcome of the forecasted events typically cannot be known. In turn, the payoff values of the underlying stock shares cannot be linked to the outcome of the event, so the traditional incentive system breaks down. Alternative payoff mechanisms then base the payoff value on the volume weighted average trading prices (LaComb et al., 2007), the last fixed price (Chan et al., 2002, Soukhoroukova and Spann, 2005), or the last fixed price when a market closes at a random point in time (Dahan et al., 2009). Despite the likely influence of different payoff mechanisms on forecasting accuracy, no empirical or comprehensive conceptual comparisons provide knowledge about the forecasting accuracy of those payoff mechanisms or their effects on participants' trading behavior.

This article conceptually and empirically compares the forecasting accuracy of the three alternative payoff mechanisms and their influence on participants' trading behavior. In essence, we attempt to identify the best of the three payoff mechanisms and determine how well it works. We organize the remainder of this paper as follows: In the next section, we introduce and discuss G1 PMs, which rely on knowledge of the actual outcome, as well as their applications and shortcomings. Thereafter, we review existing approaches for determining payoff values in G2 PMs, followed by a conceptual comparison. We subsequently present the design of our experimental study in section 4, followed by the presentation of results in section 5. We conclude with limitations and further avenues for research in section 6.

2. First Generation PMs with Actual Outcome Payoff Mechanisms

2.1. Overview

As their general premise, G1 PMs assemble participants in an online marketplace, where they trade shares of virtual stock whose values relate to the outcomes of events. For example, participants might trade shares of stock tied to the outcome of an election (e.g., "the winner is a Democrat"), such that the value of a share represents the probability or the expected value of that event (Wolfers and Zitzewitz, 2004, Wolfers and Zitzewitz, 2008). If a share of the stock "the winner is a Democrat" has a current value of $0.75 (or $75), it implies a 0.75 probability that the Democratic candidate will win the election. Participants who think the share of stock is undervalued (i.e., believe the true probability is higher) buy shares, whereas those who believe in a lower winning probability sell their shares. By expressing events as stocks, expectations about the events become tradable. The shares' final values, or *payoff values*, relate to the stock's underlying event. Therefore, if the Democratic candidate actually wins the election, every participant holding that share of stock receives $1 (or $100) per share (regardless of the final trading value of that share), and those participants who hold shares of the alternative stock "the winner is a Republican" receive $0 per share.

The theoretical foundation for PMs relies on the efficient market hypothesis (Hayek, 1945), which states that asymmetrically dispersed information can best be aggregated by a market mechanism. If the information possessed by all market participants is fully reflected in share prices, the market is efficient (Fama, 1970, Fama, 1991). In the case of efficient markets, at any point in time, market prices reflect the most accurate predictions of all market participants regarding the outcome of the event. Despite some recent evidence that PMs are not fully efficient (Foutz and Jank, 2008), the principle is still very powerful.

Different types of outcomes can be traded in PMs. The most common is the "winner takes all" (wta) market, in which shares of one or more stocks are traded and only one of the stocks' underlying events eventually is true. In this case, the shares of the winning stock are valued at $100 (or $1), and all shares of the losing stocks are valued at $0. Theoretical (Wolfers and Zitzewitz, 2008) and empirical (e.g., Cowgill et al., 2008) evidence indicates that share prices, and thus their associated forecasts, correspond to the true probabilities that an event will occur.

The second type of outcome corresponds to a linear rule, whose continuously valued payoff value depends on the actual outcome. For example, to forecast the sales of a product in the next quarter, the typical payoff value would be actual sales or a particular proportion thereof. Thus, if actual sales of the product were $50 million, a share of stock would pay out at $50 (or some other proportional reflection of the total). In turn, a current share value of $55 indicates that actual sales in the next quarter should be as high as $55 million (Spann and Skiera, 2003, Wolfers and Zitzewitz, 2004).

2.2. Applications

The first application of PMs occurred in the political environment in 1988 to forecast the winner of a presidential election (Forsythe et al., 1992). Since then, the Iowa electronic markets have run many more U.S. political stock markets (Berg et al., 2003), but there also have been applications in various other areas, including sports (e.g., Rosenbloom and Notz, 2006, Servan-Schreiber et al., 2004, Spann and Skiera, 2009), economics (Gürkaynak and Wolfers, 2005), and even medicine (Holden, 2007). In recent years, PMs have appeared more as a means for forecasting managerially relevant questions, usually in corporate settings. Ortner (1998), studying their forecasting output for project completion deadlines at Siemens, finds high forecasting accuracy. At Hewlett Packard, Chen and Plott (2002) show that market based forecasts offer much better forecasting than the company's traditional methods. One of the largest PMs, the Hollywood Stock Exchange (HSX), consistently demonstrates its strong performance in forecasting the box office sales of new Hollywood movies. Spann and Skiera (2003) find in particular that the HSX delivers at least similar and frequently better results than renowned movie experts. Elberse and Anand (2005) also use HSX data to study the effect of advertising on revenues and find a significantly positive relation. Using a large data set across different movies, these authors determine that the effect declines for lesser quality movies. Additional examples of company related success stories include Google, which has employed several different PMs to forecast business related figures, such as the number of future Gmail users (Cowgill et al., 2008). Inspired by the early success of markets such as the HSX, a growing number of large companies (e.g., Microsoft, Eli Lilly, Hewlett Packard) employ internal PMs (Kiviat, 2004).

Other research attempts to study the factors that drive prices in PMs. For example, Elberse (2007) examines the reaction of the HSX movie market to announcements of new stars in the cast and finds a significant impact on predicted sales, which implies that stars drive up the sales of movies. Foutz and Jank (2008) instead employ novel shape analysis to study the effect of price histories on forecasting accuracy and find that certain market shapes can capture phenomena such as herding, which implies that PMs are not fully efficient. In an attempt to understand trading behavior in PMs, Spann et al. (2009) show that individual participants can deliver important managerial insights as lead users in the new product development process.

2.3. *Shortcomings*

Despite these many success stories, G1 PMs have a major shortcoming: The outcome of an event must be known to determine the shares' payoff values and to correctly incentivize participants to trade and reveal their true beliefs. However, for many managerially relevant questions, outcomes may never be known (e.g., which of several alternatives to implement). This type of market, a preference market, provides an example of G2 PMs. Managerial decision making often requires a choice of one among many options (e.g., product features, design alternatives). The success of the chosen option, in theory, can be evaluated eventually, but the outcome of all remaining (not chosen) options can never be known. Idea markets further this concept by letting participants suggest their own ideas as stocks.

Another type of outcome not entirely captured by preference markets is one that can be known only at a point very distant in the future, such as when the outcome relates to the success of a long term strategic investment or decision. For example, what will the penetration of RFID enabled refrigerators in of U.S. households be in 2015? The answer will not be known for a long time (i.e. not until 2015), so G1 PM mechanisms are difficult to apply. However, by using G2 payoff mechanisms, questions of this type can potentially be answered and evaluated within the PM context.

3. Second Generation PMs with Alternative Payoff Mechanisms

3.1. General Approaches

The key challenge when dealing with G2 PMs is to replace the payoff mechanism in G1 PMs with an alternative mechanism that determines the final payoff value of the shares of each stock, independent of the outcome. Generally, this exchange could be conducted in two different ways. First, payoff values might be determined market internally by using only the data generated from the trading activity. In this case, trading actions serve as proxies for the payoff values, because every trade determines a new share price that reflects the participants' valuation of the stock. By choosing and possibly aggregating a subset of the data, one can try to determine the "true value" of the stock, which serves as payoff value. Second, payoff values might be determined externally through a proxy measure that is independent of the market's trading activity. At this place, experts could evaluate each share of stock and determine the payoff value (Graefe and Weinhardt, 2008, Soukhoroukova et al., 2008).

Several differences mark market internal and market external payoff mechanisms. The determination of market internal payoff values requires no additional effort to gather the necessary information, whereas the effort increases considerably when a group of outside experts is required. The related costs and availability of appropriate sources, as well as the aggregation of expert opinions, can impose significant difficulties. Moreover, if experts participate in markets, we must question the independence of the market and the evaluation mechanisms. Finally, expert evaluations could lead participants to predict (potentially biased) expert decisions rather than submitting their own privately held evaluations, especially if the experts and their biases are known. Therefore, we only consider market internal payoff values for G2 PMs herein.

3.2. Existing Studies

Four studies consider market internal payoff mechanisms for preference and idea markets (Chan et al., 2002, Dahan et al., 2009, LaComb et al., 2007, Soukhoroukova and Spann, 2005). They generally indicate the advantages of market based methods compared with other instruments, such as costs, scalability, and the existence of biases, yet none provides a test of external validity or forecasting accuracy. Rather, evaluations typically are based on proxy measures, such as the results of conjoint studies, surveys, or Delphi methods.

One type of G2 payoff mechanism bases the payoff on the volume weighted average price (vwap) over a certain period of time (LaComb et al., 2007):

(1) $$payoff_i^{vwap} = \frac{\sum_t p_{i,t} \cdot q_{i,t}}{\sum_t q_{i,t}}, \text{ with } time(t) \geq vwap\_start.$$

In this equation, $p_{i,t}$ denotes the price of a share of the ith stock at the tth trade, $q_{i,t}$ denotes the corresponding number of shares per trade, *vwap_start* is the point in time at which the vwap calculation starts, and *time(t)* is the point in time at which the tth trade is executed. Because the vwap includes trades over a certain period of time to determine payoff values, it attempts to reduce reliance on single trades.

An alternative G2 payoff mechanism relies on the last price at which a stock traded at a fixed and publicly known point in time, T^{fixed} (Chan et al., 2002, Soukhoroukova and Spann, 2005):

(2) $\quad payoff_i^{last\ price} = p_{i,\max(t)}$, with time$(t) \leq T^{fixed}$.

The rationale for this payoff measure derives from the efficient market hypothesis, which states that all available information at the end of the market should be reflected in the last price. Moreover, the concept is easily conveyed to and understood by all market participants.

A third G2 alternative, similar to the previous measure, uses the final trading price but closes the market at a random point in time (Dahan et al., 2009). Therefore, T^{random} is between two prespecified points in time, $random\_start$ and $random\_end$, and the last price random close can be computed as:

(3) $\quad payoff_i^{last\ price\ random\ close} = p_{i,\max(t)}$, with
$\quad\quad$ time$(t) \leq T^{random} \wedge random\_start \leq T^{random} \leq random\_end$.

This mechanism thus attempts to avoid last minute price manipulations.

Although these three G2 payoff mechanisms appear in previous studies, their forecasting accuracy has not been compared. Moreover, all payoff mechanisms aim at eliciting participants' true beliefs about the event, but no investigations address whether they influence trading behavior systematically. We focus on these two issues.

4. Conceptual Comparison of Payoff Mechanisms

4.1. Expected Accuracy of G1 and G2 Payoff Mechanisms

Wolfers and Zitzewitz (2004) cite three reasons G1 PMs with actual outcome payoff mechanisms should perform well: They provide (1) incentives to seek information, (2) incentives for truthful information revelation, and (3) an algorithm for aggregating diverse opinions. The essential idea of PMs is that updates of existing information earn rewards when the new information is more accurate than existing information but penalties when the new information is less accurate. Ultimately, the payoff value relates to the occurrence of a particular event, so its occurrence (or non occurrence) determines how much participants earn. In turn, both public and private information should be incorporated into prices.

In contrast, the alternative payoff mechanisms — volume weighted average price (vwap), last price, and last price random close — do not depend on the actual outcome, and the payoff values might be completely independent of the "true" outcome. In theory, this shift should alter the trading strategies in the markets. That is, in G1 PMs in which the payoff values are based on the actual outcome, participants' investment decisions should rely on the expected actual outcomes, whereas in G2 PMs, participants must predict the vwap or last traded price. Therefore, they have no incentive to reveal their private information, because doing so does not necessarily earn them rewards from the mechanism. A form of information cascade might result (Bikhchandani et al., 1992), such that private information gets underweighted and transactions instead depend on transactions by other participants. Although this informational inefficiency might occur in PMs with actual outcome payoff values (Anderson and Holt, 1997), the effect is likely larger in G2 PMs, because portfolio performance essentially depends not only on the owner's own assessments but also to a large extent on the assessments of others, that is, the majority of remaining participants. In summary, we expect G1 PMs with payoff values based on actual outcomes to be superior in terms of prediction accuracy than G2 PMs with payoff values based on alternative payoffs.

4.2. Expected Trading Behavior in G2 PMs

Alternative payoff mechanisms in G2 PMs may affect the overall prediction accuracy of the market, as well as individual participants' trading actions. However, to understand individual trading behavior, we first investigate the market mechanism, or the rule for making individual trades.

4.2.1 Market mechanisms in PMs

Most PMs employ automated market makers (AMMs) as market mechanisms, because they tend to be very illiquid (Pennock, 2004, Hanson et al., 2006). These AMMs can execute buy and sell orders at any point in time, so trading is always possible, unlike in standard continuous double auctions, which require matching between buy and sell orders.

We use Hanson's (2003, 2007) market scoring rules, the most widely used AMM, which adopt a continuous price function that sets the share price, depending on the number of shares in the market. By buying or selling shares of stocks, the participant can drive the price of the shares up or down, from an old to a new price. The mean share price that a participant pays for a certain amount of shares then is roughly in the middle between the old price and the new price. For example, assume the current share price is $50 (old price). By buying 10 (20) additional shares, a participant drives the price up to $60 ($70) (new price)[6]. However, the price paid for 10 (20) shares falls between $50 and $60 ($70) (roughly $50.5 for the first, $51.5 for the second, $59.5 for the tenth, $69.5 for the twentieth share, etc.), because the continuous price function prices every single share of stock differently. Therefore, the participant pays roughly $55 ($60) for each of the 10 (20) shares to drive the price from $50 to the new final price of $60 ($70). The trade is now described as "Buy 10 (20) at a price of $60 ($70)." We consider the new price for the description of the trade, as it is the trader's final valuation of the share, rather than the mean price paid. Moreover, the mean price paid also incorporates the old price, which in turn should not matter for the description of the current trade.

4.2.2 Trading behavior

To analyze trading behavior, we consider two aspects: myopic strategies, which focus on participants' considerations for each trade, and the resultant possible herding behavior. In vwap markets, which determine a stock's payoff value according to the volume weighted average price over a period of time, the trading period consists of two phases: a first phase when trades are not considered for the calculation of the vwap, prior to *vwap_start*, and a second phase, in which every trade gets taken into account for the vwap calculation. In theory, from a myopic point of view, trading behavior should differ significantly between these two trading phases: Every trade executed in the second phase should result in a loss for the participant if he or she executes only small trades. For illustration, consider a simple scenario: Assume a vwap trading history of 5 shares traded at a price of $50. The current price is $50 (old price). The participant then decides to buy two shares at prices $50.5 and $51.5, which drives the price, through the AMM, to $52 (new/last fixed price). On average, the participant has paid $51 for each share of stock. The current payoff

---

[6] The speed at which prices move is controlled via one parameter

(calculated by vwap) is lower than the invested capital; specifically, the vwap for this transaction (see Equation 1) equals $(5 \times \$50 + 2 \times \$52)/(5 + 2) = \$50.57$, which is lower than the $51 that was paid for each share. Therefore, there is little incentive for a participant to conduct such a transaction.

The scenario differs for trades of more shares. When buying 10 shares, for example, the price would move up to $60, and the cost for this transaction would be the mean between $50 and $60, or $55 per share. In this case, the vwap rewards the transaction because the ensuing payoff would reach as high as $(5 \times \$50 + 10 \times \$60)/(5 + 10) = \$56.67$, higher than the average invested capital of $55 per share. From a myopic view, the participant has more incentives to initiate larger price changes, which implies trading more shares, to increase the price changes and thus the price volatility. Therefore, we expect trading activity to be greater in the second trading phase, when the vwap calculation kicks in, than in the first phase. Moreover, we expect this trend to increase near the end of the markets, as the vwap gains more and more trading memory and requires larger trading quantities to alter that memory. As another potential consequence, herding might result when participants receive rewards from moving prices in the same direction.

The vwap mechanism can influence an individual participant's trading behavior, though similar effects also might occur with other G2 payoff mechanisms. In last price markets, from a myopic point of view, every trade is immediately profitable if it is the last one. When buying, for example, 10 shares of stock, the price for each share is $55 on average. Yet the last fixed price of the last trade is $60, which also represents the payoff value. These considerations are analogous to (short) sales.

When a participant has bought (sold) shares previously, it makes even more sense for him or her to buy more (sell) shares later. With every purchase (sale), a participant not only profits from the recently bought (sold) shares but also increases (decreases) the value of shares in the portfolio. Therefore, participants obtain strong rewards for their herding behavior (i.e., price moves in the same direction) near the end of the market. Trading activity thus should increase at the end of last price markets, especially the very last moments.

In contrast, we do not anticipate last minute trading in last price random close markets, because the closing time of the markets is unknown to participants. Therefore, herding behavior and last minute movements should be weaker.

5. Experimental design

We use a field experiment to test the different payoff mechanisms and compare the forecasting accuracy of G2 payoff mechanisms (G1 mechanism as a benchmark) and the impact of G2 trading mechanisms on individual trading behavior. Because we cannot assess true performance in markets with events whose outcomes will never occur, we base our experiment on forecasting events that do occur and to analyze the forecasting accuracy of the different payoff mechanisms. Prior research indicates that the type of event to be predicted may have an effect on the market outcome (Rosenbloom and Notz, 2006). Therefore, unlike most studies, which focus on one topic, we base our analyses on three different topics, namely, politics, sports, and general economic issues.

We ran experiments pertaining to these three topics in the spring term of 2008 at a major U.S. east coast university. The subjects were 78 MBA students. With three alternative payoff mechanisms to be tested and the actual outcome mechanism as a benchmark, we obtained four different types of markets. We randomly assigned each student to one of the four payoff mechanisms. Students did not participate in the same payoff mechanism more than once, to eliminate possible learning effects. Moreover, to achieve more robust results, we ran each market experiment in two replications, with each student assigned to either the first or second replication. These assignments resulted in a total of eight different markets for each topic, or 24 total different markets. Each topic consisted of nine to eleven stocks, for a total of $4 \times 2 \times (11 + 10 + 9) = 240$ single stocks (see Table 1). We used 17 winner takes all stocks and 13 linear stocks (see the Appendix).

The initial endowment of each participant consisted of $10,000 in virtual currency. After each round of the experiment, we reset participants' portfolio values to the initial values to avoid endowment effects across experiments. We added their profits (or losses) to determine their overall ranking. The top 10% of all students received 110% of course credit (equivalent to an A+); the top 90% to 60% received 100% of course credit (i.e., an A); those ranked in the 60–20 percentiles received 90% (i.e. a B); and the lowest 20% received 80% (i.e., a C). Luckner and Weinhardt (2007) show that such a rank order tournament incentive scheme leads to the best results in terms of prediction accuracy in play money markets. We also offered four gift certificates with values up to $50; however, we believe that the course credits were a much greater incentive than the promise of gift certificates. All students had this information before the start of the experiments, which means it was transparent to all participants that they had to maximize their portfolio values to obtain a high standing in the field. Participants also were instructed repeatedly to remain aware of the individual payoff mechanisms orally, by e-mail, and within the trading system at different places, on the main screen, and in the descriptions of the stocks.

Factor	Number of Levels	Specification
Topics	3 (1)	• Primaries on March 3, 2008 (also experts) • "Final Four" NCAA basketball games on April 5, 2008 • Economic events in or at the end of April
Payoff mechanism	4 (1)	• Based on actual outcome (also experts) • Based on vwap of last 48 hours • Based on last fixed price • Based on last fixed price with random close of market (within 4 hours of close of all markets)
Replications	2 (1)	• Each market with 9–10 student participants (24 expert participants)
Total number of markets	3 · 4 · 2 = **24** (1 · 1 · 1 = **1**)	
Stocks	10 on average per market (11)	• Overall 17 winner takes all and 13 linear stocks (4 winner takes all, 7 linear)
Total number of stocks	24 · 10 = **240** (1 · 11 = **11**)	

Table 1: Experimental design (expert markets in parentheses)

The calculation of the vwap took place during the second half of the trading period, specifically, the last 48 hours, which is an appropriate period for two reasons: It is *short enough* to let the market prices move away from the initial starting prices but *long enough* that prices are not moved easily by single trades. In the last price random close markets, they closed at a random point in time during the last 4 hours of trading. Both time spans were transparent on the Web site for all affected participants.

To establish the actual outcome markets' validity as a benchmark, we created another, self contained market for the first topic (election primaries) with 11 stocks, which consisted of 24 experts from political consultancy firms across the United States. Although the only extrinsic incentive for the participants was a $100 gift certificate for the winner, we believe that their displays in the rankings were sufficient incentive for them to perform well, due to peer pressure. The payoff values reflect the actual outcomes of the events. As software, we used a self developed trading platform that we tested in several previous experiments and field studies.

We also allowed for the short selling of shares, which, in conjunction with the market mechanism (i.e. the AMM), enabled participants to move stock prices in their desired direction at any point in time. The markets were completely identical, except for the payoff mechanisms and their descriptions. For example, the descriptions of the stock "A margin greater than 10 percent by either Clinton or Obama in Ohio" were as follows for the markets with these respective payoff values:

- *Actual outcome:* "The price of this share of stock denotes the probability that the margin of votes by either Obama or Clinton is greater than 10 percentage points in the Ohio primaries [...] After the elections, the stock will cash out after the primaries at $100 if the margin is more than 10 points, else at 0$. [...] The market closes Monday, March 3rd, 8 PM."

- *Volume weighted average price:* "The price of this share of stock denotes the probability that the margin by either Obama or Clinton is greater than 10 percentage points in the Ohio primaries. [...] The stock will cash out at the **volume weighted average price**, determined between Saturday, March 1st, 8PM, and Monday, March 3rd, 8PM."

- *Last price:* "The price of this share of stock denotes the probability that the margin by either Obama or Clinton is greater than 10 percentage points in the Ohio primaries. [...] The stock will cash out at the **last fixed price** before the close of the markets on Monday, March 3rd, 8 PM."

- *Last price random close:* "The price of this share of stock denotes the probability that the margin by either Obama or Clinton is greater than 10 percentage points in the Ohio primaries. [...] The stock will cash out at the **last fixed price** before the close of the markets. The markets will close at a **random point in time** on Monday, March 3rd, between 4 PM and 8 PM."

6. Results

We next discuss the results of our experiments. Because we have both winner takes all stocks, whose share prices range from 0 to 100, and linear stocks, whose share prices can range between two arbitrary numbers, we linearly normalize the final price of stocks with continuous payoffs in the range 0–100. For example, we normalize the final price of a stock with a continuous payoff of $55, which traded between $40 and $60, to a price of $75 (= ($55 − $40)/($60 − $40)). This normalization enables us to examine both types of stocks simultaneously.

6.1. Forecast Accuracy

We investigate the forecast accuracy of the different payoff mechanisms according to their mean absolute forecast errors (MAE), which equals the absolute difference between the forecast and the true outcome (see Table 2).

Payoff Mechanism	Actual outcome with Students	Actual outcome with experts	Vwap	Last price	Last price random close
Topic 1 (Politics)					
MAE	18.15	19.72	30.70	23.39	31.66
Std. error	3.62	7.27	5.03	4.21	5.10
N	22	11	22	22	22
Topic 2 (Sports)					
MAE	31.22		27.77	30.49	29.30
Std. error	6.50		6.31	6.66	5.71
N	20		20	20	20
Topic 3 (Economy)					
MAE	39.28		46.05	48.37	41.83
Std. error	6.34		6.93	5.85	5.70
N	18		18	18	18
All					
MAE	28.85		34.33	33.25	33.92
Std. error	3.37		3.63	3.49	3.24
N	60		60	60	60

Table 2: Mean absolute errors across topics

To evaluate the forecasting accuracy of the student markets and confirm them as a valid benchmark, we compare their forecasting accuracy to that of the expert markets, which considered 11 stocks in the first topic. The actual outcome student markets performed no worse than the expert markets; in fact, they performed slightly better, with a MAE of 18.15 compared with a MAE of 19.72 for the expert markets. However, the difference is not significant (paired t-test, paired for each stock with the expert markets and the average of the two actual outcome market stocks), which suggests that the forecasting accuracy by the students is not significantly different than that by the experts.

When comparing all payoff mechanisms, we find that the actual outcome markets (i.e., with G1 mechanisms) perform best, which is not surprising and fits our hypothesis. The best G2 performance comes from the last price markets, with an error of 33.25 (absolute difference 4.40); the vwap and last price random close markets perform only marginally worse, with MAE of 34.33 and 33.92, respectively.

In line with results obtained by Rosenbloom and Notz (2006), we find that the forecasting accuracy varies between different topics. That is, error for the second topic (sports) is lower for the G2 markets than for the actual outcome (G1) markets.[7] In contrast, for the two other topics, the actual outcome markets outperformed the alternative markets, with an absolute difference of at least of 5.24 percentage points (significant at least at the 10% level, paired t-test) in the first topic and 2.55 (not significant, paired t-test) in the third.

Stock Type	Linear Stocks				Winner Takes All Stocks			
Payoff mechanism	Actual outcome	Vwap	Last price	Last price random close	Actual outcome	Vwap	Last price	Last price random close
MAE	14.01	19.78	18.77	17.71	48.25	53.36	52.19	55.12
Std. error	2.69	3.54	3.24	2.50	4.74	4.90	4.74	3.84
N	34	34	34	34	26	26	26	26

Table 3: Mean absolute errors across stock types

Because we consider two different types of stock (linear versus winner takes all), we also analyze them separately as their type may have different effects on forecasting accuracy. The error of a winner takes all stock can be fairly high, even when the forecast is correct. For example, if the true probability of an event is 51:49 and the market correctly predicts a 51% probability, the error can be as great as 49 percentage points. In our experiment, the actual outcome mechanism markets perform better for both stock types, with errors of 14.01 for linear stocks and 48.25 for winner takes all stocks. However, the results for the G2 payoff mechanisms are less consistent. The last price random close markets perform best for linear stocks, with an error of 17.71,[8] and they perform worst for winner takes all stocks, with an error of 55.12.[9] In the vwap and last price markets, the latter outperform the former

---

[7] Specifically, 27.77, 30.49, and 29.30, compared with 31.22, which is not significant according to the paired t-test.
[8] Not significant compared with the actual outcome markets, 10%, paired t-test.
[9] Not significant compared with the actual outcome markets, 10% level.

for both stock types with MAEs of 18.77[10] versus 19.78,[11] respectively, for winner takes all and 52.19 versus 53.36,[12] respectively, for linear.

To investigate the impact of different payoff mechanisms on forecasting accuracy while controlling for stock type and topic, we next set up the following linear model. The dependent variable is the (natural) logarithm of the absolute error, plus 1[13]:

(4)
$$\begin{aligned}e_{i,p,r} = &\beta_0 \\&+ \beta_1 \cdot DV\_linear_i + \\&+ \beta_2 \cdot DV\_topic\_2_i \\&+ \beta_3 \cdot DV\_topic\_3_i \\&+ \beta_4 \cdot DV\_vwap_i \\&+ \beta_5 \cdot DV\_last\_price_i \\&+ \beta_6 \cdot DV\_last\_price\_random\_close_i \\&+ \mu_{i,p,r},\end{aligned}$$

where

$e_{i,p,r}$: dependent variable, $e_{i,p,r} = \ln(abs\_error_{i,p,r} + 1)$, of the ith stock, payoff mechanism p, and the rth replication.

DV_linear_i: dummy variable, equal to 1 if the ith stock type is linear and 0 if stock type is winner takes all.

$DV\_topic\_X_i$: dummy variable, equal to 1 if the ith stock is part of topic X and 0 otherwise.

DV_P_i: dummy variable, equal to 1 if the ith stock's payoff mechanism is P and 0 otherwise.

$\mu_{i,p,r}$: residual of the ith stock with payoff mechanism p and the rth replication.

We control for topics (two dummy variables), because they likely influence the forecasting accuracy of the markets. We have a total of N = 240 observations to estimate our model.

---

[10] Significant at 5%.
[11] Significant at 10%.
[12] Neither is significant at 10%.
[13] Absolute errors are not normally distributed, requiring the logarithmic transformation and, because of the existence of zero values, the addition of 1 to all absolute errors.

	Model	
	β	sig.
Constant	3.413	(0.000) ***
DV_linear	-1.242	(0.000) ***
DV_topic_2 (sports)	0.075	(0.562)
DV_topic_3 (economy)	0.491	(0.000) ***
DV_vwap	0.256	(0.096) *
DV_last-price	0.227	(0.138)
DV_last-price-random-close	0.303	(0.049) **
R^2 / adj.	0.413 / 0.398	
F-value	27.333 ***	
N	240	

Table 4: Regression results for influence on absolute forecasting error
(*: significant at 0.1 level; **: significant at 0.05 level; ***: significant at 0.01 level.

The results in Table 4 show that linear stocks have a significantly lower absolute forecasting error than do winner takes all stocks, as we have suggested. Also, the outcomes for the economy (topic 3) are less accurate than those for the remaining topics. Regarding the different payoff mechanisms, the last price mechanisms perform as well as actual outcome markets, which is quite remarkable. For the other two alternative mechanisms, vwap and last price random close, the prediction accuracy decreases (though the difference in the results is not significant at the 10% level).

6.2. Trading Behavior

As we noted, we expect different payoff mechanisms to have different effects on participants' trading behavior. We investigate whether the data support this expectation. To examine whether alternative payoff mechanisms cause a systematic deviation in trading behavior, we compare this behavior with that of participants in actual outcome markets. Assuming that G1 markets produce "normal" trading behavior, we investigate the G2 deviations, controlling for stock and topic specific effects, both of which affect forecast accuracy. By computing pair wise differences of the prices and cumulative traded quantities between actual and alternative mechanisms, we can filter out effects such as forecasting difficulty or general lack of knowledge about certain events.

6.2.1 Price difference between G1 and G2 markets

We compute the mean difference of prices between alternate (G2) and actual (G1) markets for each stock and each replication, as follows:

$$(5) \quad \Delta price_{p,z} = \frac{1}{30 \cdot 2} \sum_{i=1}^{30} \sum_{r=1}^{2} \left(p_{i,p,r,z} - \frac{p_{i,actual,1,z} + p_{i,actual,2,z}}{2} \right),$$

where $p_{i,p,r,z}$ is the price of the ith stock with a payoff mechanism p at the rth replication at time z. We compute the mean differences (black solid lines) and corresponding 95% confidence bounds (dashed lines) for each payoff mechanism, as we show in Figure 1. Figure 1, in the first half of the trading period, when the vwap calculation has not yet started, the mean difference falls below the horizontal zero level line. This difference signifies that the prices of the alternative payoff markets are less than those of the actual outcome markets, though not significantly. (Note that the confidence bounds include zero.) As soon as the vwap calculation starts, the vwap share prices start to increase and then stay above the actual market prices, though again not significantly until the last eight trading hours. This result is in line with our conceptual considerations; we expected a strong movement of prices in the second half of the trading phase. Although in theory, prices could move in either direction, we clearly determine that prices rise significantly. In the last trading hours in particular, we find that vwap markets exhibit a type of herding behavior, which is not limited to the last minutes of trading but rather starts hours before the close. This observation of overpricing mirrors a previous vwap study (LaComb et al., 2007, Table 2), in which most share prices were higher than the starting prices, even with a continuous double auction, rather than an AMM, as a market mechanism.

In last price markets (middle panel), we find that prices are never significantly different from actual payoff market prices. Rather, they are slightly underpriced most of time, with the exception of the last few trading hours, when prices increase and average almost the same as the actual payoff markets prices. We expected this behavior to be much more extreme, such that prices would move even more steeply toward the end. We therefore analyze last minute trading further subsequently.

Finally, in the last price random close markets, the effect is similar. Over time, prices do not differ significantly from actual outcome market prices. However, as in the last price markets, prices increase in the final trading hours. We did not anticipate this increase in theory, but herding behavior seems to have commenced a few hours before the close of the markets.

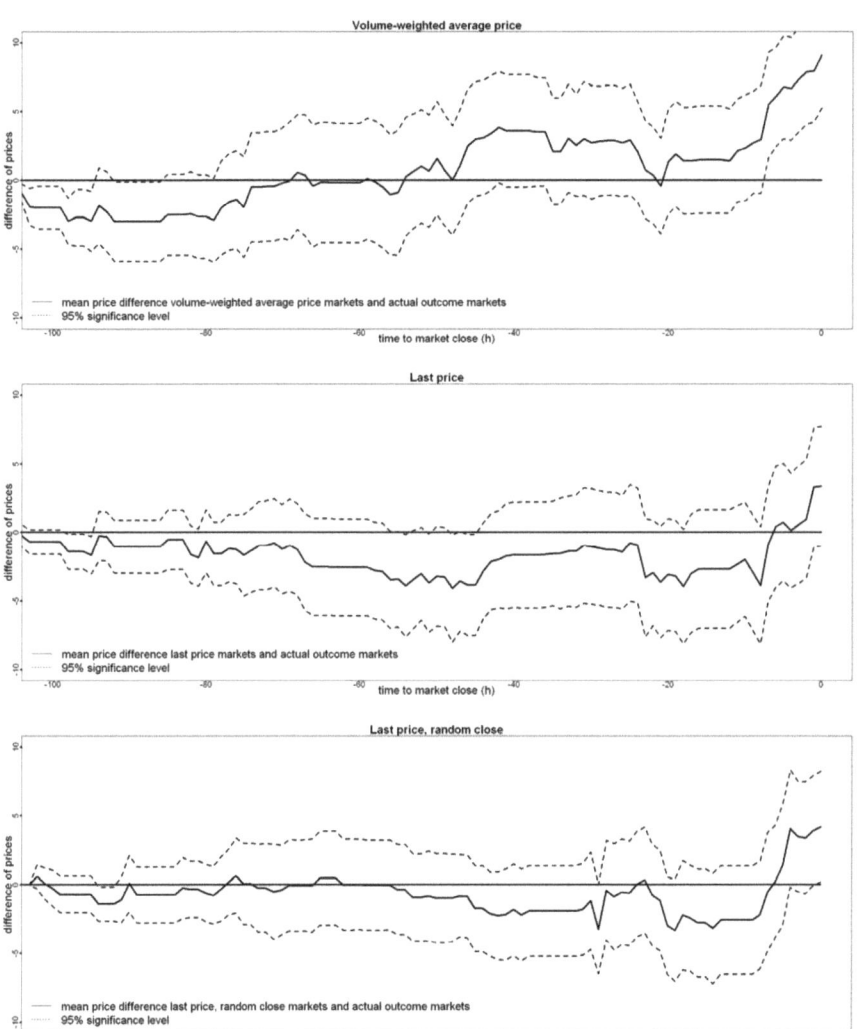

Figure 1: Differences across time of prices between markets with alternative payoff mechanisms and markets with actual outcomes.
Notes: Dashed lines signify 95% confidence intervals.

6.2.2 Trading volume difference between G1 and G2 markets

Similar to our analysis of the mean differences of prices, we study the mean differences of cumulative trading quantities to determine the trading behavior of market participants. We denote $Q_{i,p,r,t}$ as the cumulative number of traded shares of the ith stock, with payoff mechanism p and in the rth replication until a point in time z as follows:

$$(6) \quad \Delta traded\_shares_{p,z} = \frac{1}{30 \cdot 2} \sum_{i=1}^{30} \sum_{r=1}^{2} \left(Q_{i,p,r,z} - \frac{Q_{i,actual,1,z} + Q_{i,actual,2,z}}{2} \right).$$

We depict the results in Figure 2. In vwap markets, a significantly higher number of shares gets traded (cf. actual markets), and the effect intensifies toward the end of the trading period. These results support our expectations; we stipulated that trading intensity should be higher after the start of the vwap calculations because larger trades would be more profitable for participants.

A weaker effect emerges for the last price and last price random close markets. Trading activity is constantly higher than in actual outcome markets; however, this effect is not significant (the confidence bounds include zero). This result is what we expected, because from a myopic point of view, every trade should be profitable (without inventory considerations). However, participants seem to input their beliefs early into prices, despite alleged downsides when it comes to their evaluations.

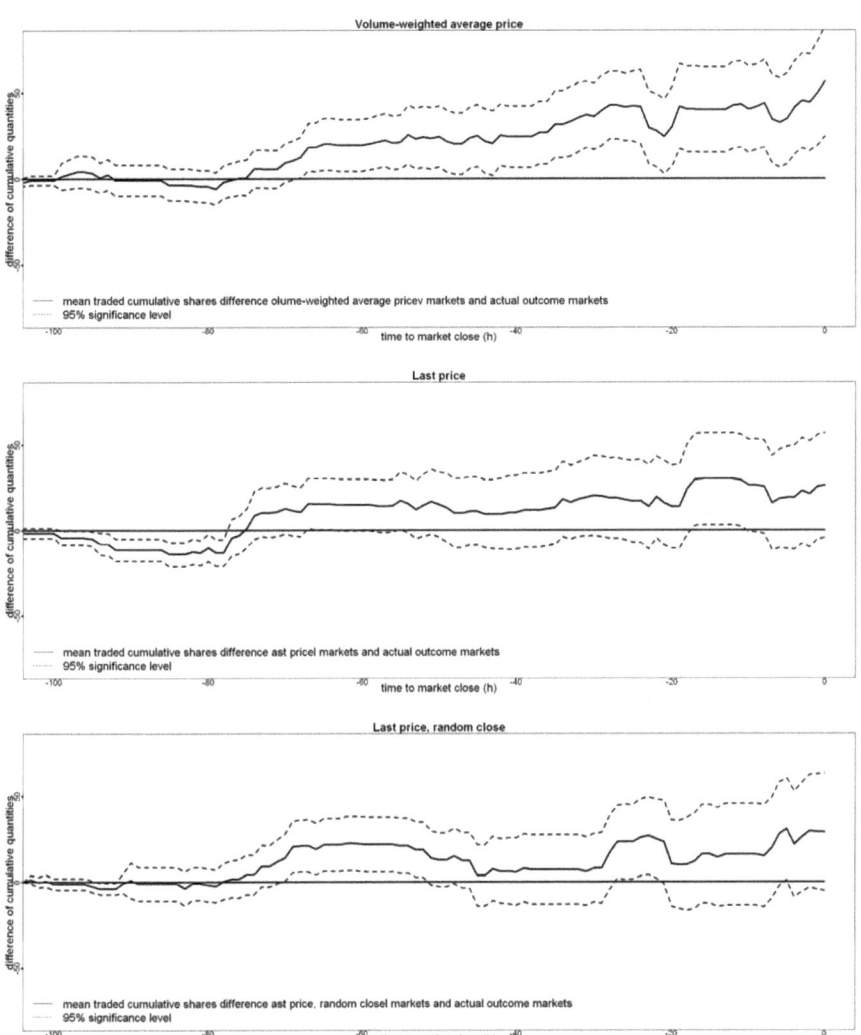

Figure 2: Differences across time of cumulative trading quantities between markets with alternative payoff mechanisms and markets with actual outcomes.
Notes: Dashed lines signify 95% confidence intervals.

6.3. Last Minute Trading

We hypothesized that last minute trades, just before the close of the markets, should particularly happen in last price markets. To uncover this behavior, we focus on the last two hours before the close of the markets and determine the cumulative percentage of all trades and cumulative percentage of all traded shares.

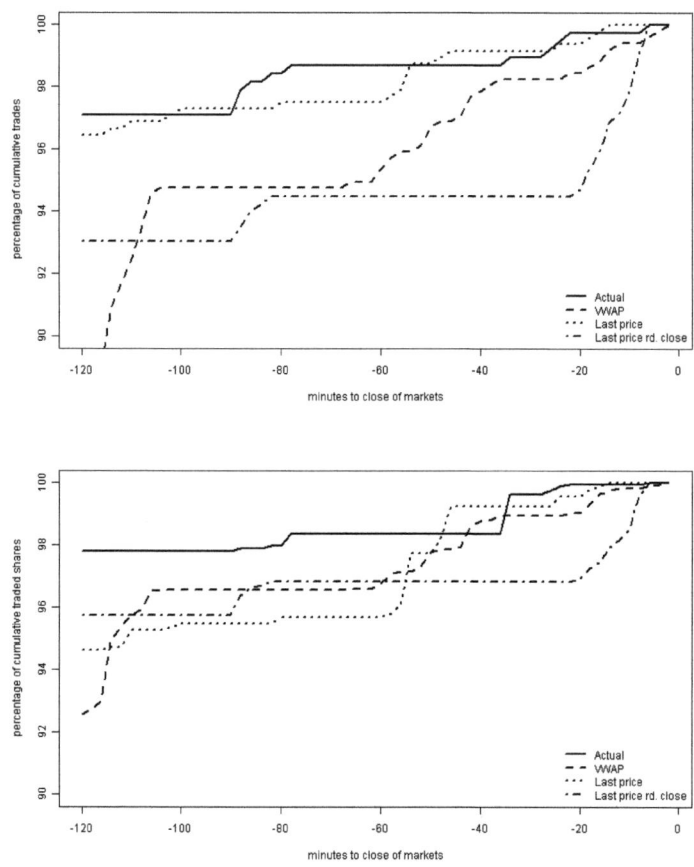

Figure 3: Cumulative number of trades (upper figure) and traded shares (lower figure) in the last minutes of markets with alternative payoff mechanisms and markets with actual outcomes

As Figure 3 reveals, few trades occur and few shares are traded in the actual outcome markets, because 98% of all trades take place more than two hours before the close. Thus, we cannot detect any particular last minute trading activity for this payoff mechanism. In contrast, the vwap payoffs exhibit considerable trading during the two last hours. Two hours before the close, only 87% of all trades had been executed, and 93% of shares were traded.

These numbers rather consistently climb to 100%, though we observe no very last minute trading.

Although we did not expect this behavior in the last price markets, we do not find any very last minute trading (dotted line). Two hours before the close, more than 96% of trades had been executed, and more than 94% of shares were traded. Surprisingly, during the very last minutes of trading, we again cannot detect any high trading actions.

Also unexpectedly, we detect the highest very last minute trading behavior in the last price random close markets. That is, 20 minutes before the close of the markets, only 94% of all trades had been executed, and 96% of all shares traded, which is relatively low compared with the other markets. In this case, because the markets close randomly, it appears that constant trading took place in the last trading hours, and the participants appeared to hope for the markets to close after they traded their respective stocks.

7. Conclusion

Although so called "first generation" (G1) PMs have superior forecasting accuracy, their usage remains limited to forecasting events whose outcomes can be determined in the short or medium term. We instead investigate whether a new type of PMs, which we label "second generation" (G2) PMs, can determine forecasts of events that either never occur or only occur in the long term. By experimenting with three different topics that require forecasts of actual events, we (1) obtain a benchmark, namely, G1 PMs with payoff values based on the actual outcome, and (2) for the first time, compare the forecast accuracy of alternative G2 payoff mechanisms.

Markets in which the shares' payoff values are based on the last fixed price only perform 4.4 percentage points worse on average than PMs whose payoff values are based on the actual outcome. Markets with alternative payoff mechanisms should perform worse than actual payoff mechanisms, yet this absolute difference of error is surprisingly low. This finding is particularly notable because G1 PMs consistently have shown superior accuracy compared with the alternative instruments. Also surprisingly, the other alternative payoff mechanisms, vwap and last price random close, perform only slightly worse than the last price mechanism.

Our results are remarkable, considering the conceptual disadvantages of the G2 payoff mechanisms. In the vwap payoff, we might expect participants to trade extensively during the time the vwap is being determined, to influence prices in their desired direction. However, prices did not differ significantly from those of the benchmark until the last few hours. We also expected herding behavior in last price markets, especially right before the close of the markets, but surprisingly, we could not detect any.

In summary, this study supports the use of G2 PMs, as employed by Chan et al. (2002), Soukhoroukova and Spann (2005), Dahan et al. (2009), and LaComb et al. (2007). Moreover, we reveal that using experts to determine payoff values (Graefe and Weinhardt, 2008, Soukhoroukova et al., 2008), which can be costly, difficult, and biased, may not be required for G2 PM applications. This study therefore encourages further thinking about new application areas for G2 PMs. The problems related to the use of alternative payoff mechanisms are much less severe than what might be expected, and the particular choice of any available payoff mechanisms does not notably influence the results. Thus, G2 PMs seem to offer a promising tool to support new product development through preference or idea markets, because they can tap the collective intelligence of a crowd.

References

Anderson, L. R. & Holt, C. A. (1997) Information Cascades in the Laboratory. *American Economic Review,* 87 (5), 847-862.

Berg, J., Forsythe, R., Nelson, F. & Rietz, T. (2003) Results from a Dozen Years of Election Futures Markets Research. In Plott, C. & Smith, V. (Eds.) *Handbook of Experimental Economic Results.* Amsterdam, Elsevier.

Bikhchandani, S., Hirshleifer, D. & Welch, I. (1992) A Theory of Fads, Fashion, Custom, and Cultural Change as Informational Cascades. *Journal of Political Economy,* 100 (5), 992-1026.

Chan, N., Dahan, E., Kim, A., Lo, A. & Poggio, T. (2002) Securities Trading of Concepts (STOC). *Working Paper, Massachusetts Institute of Technology.*

Chen, K.-Y. & Plott, C. R. (2002) Information Aggregation Mechanisms: Concept, Design and Implementation for a Sales Forecasting Problem. *Working Paper, California Institute of Technology.*

Cowgill, B., Wolfers, J. & Zitzewitz, E. (2008) Using Prediction Markets to Track Information Flows: Evidence from Google. *Working Paper, Dartmouth College.*

Dahan, E. & Hauser, J. R. (2002) The Virtual Customer. *Journal of Product Innovation Management,* 19 (5), 332-353.

Dahan, E., Soukhoroukova, A. & Spann, M. (2007) New Product Development 2.0: Preference Markets. How Scalable Securities Markets Identify Winning Product Concepts & Attributes. *Journal of Product Innovation Management, forthcoming.*

Elberse, A. (2007) The Power of Stars: Do Star Actors Drive the Success of Movies? *Journal of Marketing,* 71 (4), 102-120.

Elberse, A. & Anand, B. N. (2005) The Effectiveness of Pre-Release Advertising for Motion Pictures: An Empirical Investigation Using a Simulated Market. *Information Economics and Policy,* 19 (3-4), 319-343.

Fama, E. F. (1970) Efficient Capital Markets: A Review of Theory and Empirical Work. *Journal of Finance,* 25 (2), 383-417.

Fama, E. F. (1991) Efficient Capital Markets: II. *Journal of Finance,* 46 (5), 1575-1617.

Forsythe, R., Nelson, F., Neumann, G. R. & Wright, J. (1992) Anatomy of an Experimental Political Stock Market. *American Economic Review,* 82 (5), 1142-1161.

Forsythe, R., Rietz, T. A. & Ross, T. W. (1999) Wishes, Expectations and Actions: A Survey on Price Formation in Election Stock Markets. *Journal of Economic Behavior & Organization,* 39 (1), 83-110.

Foutz, N. & Jank, W. (2008) The Wisdom of Crowds: Pre-release Forecasting via Functional Shape Analysis of the Online Virtual Stock Market. Working Paper, University of Maryland.

Graefe, A. & Weinhardt, C. (2008) Long-term Forecasting with Prediction Markets — A Field Experiment on Applicability and Expert Confidence. *Journal of Prediction Markets,* 2 (2), 71-92.

Gürkaynak, R. & Wolfers, J. (2005) Macroeconomic Derivatives: An Initial Analysis of Market-Based Macro Forecasts, Uncertainty, and Risk. In Pissarides, C. & Frankel, J. (Eds.) *NBER International Seminar on Macroeconomics.* NBER.

Hanson, R., Oprea, R. & Porter, D. (2006) Information Aggregation and Manipulation in an Experimental Market. *Journal of Economic Behavior and Organization,* 60 (4), 449-459.

Hayek, F. A. v. (1945) The Use of Knowledge in Society. *American Economic Review,* 35 (4), 519-530.

Holden, C. (2007) Bird Flu Futures. *Science,* 315, 1345.

Kiviat, B. (2004) The End of Management? *TIME, Inside Business.* July 12.

LaComb, C. A., Barnett, J. A. & Pan, Q. (2007) The Imagination Market. *Information Systems Frontiers,* 9 (2-3), 245-256.

Luckner, S. & Weinhardt, C. (2007) How to Pay Traders in Information Markets? Results from a Field Experiment. *Journal of Prediction Markets,* 1 (2), 1-10.

Ortner, G. (1998) Forecasting Markets — An Industrial Application. *Working Paper, TU Vienna.*

Pennock, D. M. (2004) A Dynamic Pari-Mutuel Market for Hedging, Wagering, and Information Aggregation. *ACM Conference on Electronic Commerce.* New York.

Rosenbloom, E. S. & Notz, W. W. (2006) Statistical Tests of Real-Money versus Play-Money Prediction Markets. *Electronic Markets,* 16 (1), 63-69.

Servan-Schreiber, E., Wolfers, J., Pennock, D. M. & Galebach, B. (2004) Prediction Markets: Does Money Matter? *Electronic Markets,* 14 (3), 243-251.

Soukhoroukova, A. & Spann, M. (2005) New Product Development with Internet-based Information Markets: Theory and Empirical Application. *13th European Conference on Information Systems (ECIS).* Regensburg.

Soukhoroukova, A., Spann, M. & Skiera, B. (2008) Creating and Evaluating New Product Ideas with Idea Markets. *Working Paper, University of Passau.*

Spann, M., Ernst, H., Skiera, B. & Soll, J. H. (2009) Identification of Lead Users for Consumer Products via Virtual Stock Markets. *Journal of Product Innovation Management,* 26 (3), 322-335.

Spann, M. & Skiera, B. (2003) Internet-Based Virtual Stock Markets for Business Forecasting. *Management Science,* 49 (10), 1310-1326.

Spann, M. & Skiera, B. (2009) Sports Forecasting: A Comparison of the Forecast Accuracy of Prediction Markets, Betting Odds and Tipsters. *Journal of Forecasting,* 28 (1), 55-77.

Wolfers, J. & Zitzewitz, E. (2004) Prediction Markets. *Journal of Economic Perspectives,* 18 (2), 107-126.

Wolfers, J. & Zitzewitz, E. (2008) Interpreting Prediction Market Prices as Probabilities. *NBER Working Paper #12200, University of Pennsylvania.*

Appendix

Question/Stock	Stock Type	Min. Value	Max. Value	Actual Outcome
Topic 1 (Politics)				
A margin greater than 10 percent by either Clinton or Obama in OH	wta	0	100	100
Obama sweeps 03/04/2008 primaries	wta	0	100	0
Edwards endorses before or on the day of the election	wta	0	100	0
Clinton suspends or drops out of the race on 3/4/08	wta	0	100	0
% of popular votes Clinton gets in OH	linear	0	100	54
% of women votes Clinton gets in OH	linear	0	100	57
% of men votes Clinton gets in OH	linear	0	100	50
% of African American votes Obama gets in OH	linear	0	100	89
% of White votes Obama gets in OH	linear	0	100	34
% of popular votes McCain gets in OH	linear	0	100	60
Number of states × 10 Clinton wins on 3/4/08	linear	0	40	30
Topic 2 (Sports)				
Memphis wins against UCLA	wta	0	100	100
UNC wins against Kansas	wta	0	100	0
3-pt field goal shooting percentage of Memphis in Memphis-UCLA game	linear	0	100	33.33
Overall shooting percentage of UCLA in Memphis-UCLA game	linear	0	100	37.5
Percent of Memphis rebounds out of total rebounds in Memphis-UCLA game	linear	0	100	54.55
Memphis-UCLA game's top scorer is from UCLA	wta	0	100	0
Free throw percentage of UNC in game UNC-Kansas	linear	0	100	86.7
Percent of Kansas turnovers out of total turnovers in game UNC-Kansas	linear	0	100	51.35
Percent of UNC fouls out of total fouls in game UNC-Kansas	linear	0	100	40
UNC-Kansas game's top scorer is from Kansas	wta	0	100	100
Topic 3 (Economy)				
Unemployment rate in April times 10	linear	40	60	50

Consumer Price Index (CPI) surpasses 4.8% in April	wta	0	100	0
Dow Jones at end of April divided by 100	linear	100	140	120.82
Euro-Dollar exchange rate is above $1.60 at end of April	wta	0	100	0
Microsoft has taken over Yahoo! by the end of April	wta	0	100	0
Crude Oil Spot Market Price at end of April	linear	100	140	113.7
Eastman Kodak's Q1 earnings are positive	wta	0	100	0
Sun Inc.'s earnings per share in Q3 of the fiscal year 2008 in cents	linear	10	30	10
Justice department approves Delta/Northwest merger by the end of April	wta	0	100	0

Table A1: Questions/stocks in experiment

Notes: wta = winner takes all.

An Empirical Investigation of the Forecast Accuracy of Play-Money Prediction Markets and Professional Betting Markets

Christian Slamka[1], Stefan Luckner[2], Thomas Seemann[3], Jan Schröder[2]

[1] School of Business and Economics, Goethe-University Frankfurt
[2] Institute of Information Systems and Management, Universität Karlsruhe (TH)
[3] Institute of Business Administration, University of Erlangen-Nuremberg

Abstract

Prediction markets have proven high forecasting performance in many areas such as politics, sports and business related fields compared to traditional instruments such as polls or expert opinions. The advantage of real-money prediction markets is to provide participants with a clear incentive to reveal their true opinion on the outcome of an event. However, it is to date unclear whether play-money prediction markets, where participants cannot suffer any losses, perform well compared to other, more strongly incentivized instruments. Thus, the goal of this paper is to compare the forecast accuracy of play-money prediction markets with that of instruments with a monetary incentive to make as accurate predictions as possible, namely fixed odds betting.

We present the results of an empirical study that compares the forecast accuracy of a play-money prediction market for the FIFA World Cup 2006 to predictions derived from odds issued by two professional betting companies. Additionally, we compare the prediction market with two more benchmarks, namely the FIFA world ranking which is based on historic data and a random predictor. We find that the play-money prediction markets for the FIFA World Cup are about as accurate as betting markets. Moreover, the prediction markets clearly outperform the FIFA world ranking as well as the random predictions.

Keywords: prediction markets, forecast accuracy, sports forecasting, betting

1. Introduction

The emergence of the Internet within the last decade has not only made many services ubiquitously available for companies around the globe, but has also created the possibility for users to share and exchange their knowledge with like minded people. Besides the simple exchange of knowledge that can be implemented in a rather informal and scarcely structured way, more sophisticated information systems like prediction markets (PMs) provide mechanisms that let users express their opinions on the outcomes of future events by the exchange of stocks. Modern IS designs which allow systems to scale up in terms of number of users, number of future events or trading frequency (e.g., Soukhoroukova and Spann, 2005) have enhanced the accessibility of such knowledge exchanges. Nowadays, the restriction of a physical meeting of participants does not hold any more. Moreover, due to the ubiquity of IS and access to it, new information is quickly dispersed, allowing for an instant reaction to events (Elberse, 2007, Slamka et al., 2008).

The basic idea of PMs is to trade virtual stocks on an electronic market whose payoffs are tied to the outcome of uncertain future events. For example, a stock can be tied to the outcome of a soccer match, paying off one (virtual) currency unit if the stock's underlying team wins. Although the final payoffs of stocks are unknown during the trading period, rational and risk neutral traders sell stocks if they consider the stocks to be overvalued and buy stocks if they consider the stocks to be undervalued (Glosten and Milgrom, 1985). As a result, the trading price reflects the traders' aggregated beliefs about the likelihood of the future event. Market prices can thus be interpreted as predictions (Forsythe et al., 1995). The theoretical justification of regarding market prices as estimates of the outcome of future events is founded in the Hayek hypothesis (Hayek, 1945). It states that asymmetrically dispersed information is best aggregated using a price mechanism. Moreover, if all the available information is reflected in the market prices, the market is informationally efficient (Fama, 1970, Fama, 1991).

Accurate forecasts are essential in many areas such as business, sports or weather forecasting, and PMs are considered to provide a way to improve forecasting accuracy (Spann and Skiera, 2003, Servan-Schreiber et al., 2004) compared to traditional forecasts such as expert predictions, polls or surveys. Good performance has also been demonstrated in corporate environments (Chen and Plott, 2002, Ortner, 1997, Plott, 2000). Thus, it is not surprising that several prominent PMs such as the Iowa Electronic Markets, TradeSports, NewsFutures or the Hollywood Stock Exchange have emerged. Furthermore, several major companies such as Hewlett Packard, Google, or Microsoft are running internal PMs for company specific predictions (Kiviat, 2004).

However, the comparison of the forecast accuracy of PMs with traditional methods to date, although reasonable under practical considerations, is associated with some drawbacks. In surveys or polls for example, the forecasting accuracy is strongly dependent on the representative choice of subjects, their veridic answers to questions and the choice of statistics (Berg et al., 2001). In PMs, on the other hand, participants do not need to be selected representatively and are incentivized to reveal their true expectation about the outcome (Berg et al., 2001). Also, when questioning experts or using business meetings, which include usually at least one expert, the incentive to give correct predictions about the outcome of an event is low as experts are not explicitly rewarded or punished in monetary terms for their given predictions (e.g., Sunstein, 2006). Thus, experts are not incentivized to reveal their private information. However, in real-money PMs, the financial success of participants is directly tied to the ability to make accurate predictions, providing them with incentives to reveal their private information.

In this paper we are interested in a comparison of the forecast accuracy of play-money PMs with a forecasting instrument where the forecaster is clearly incentivized to reveal his most accurate prediction on the outcome. In fixed odds betting, which we choose as our primary benchmark, odds on which participants can bet money are set by the betting company. In order to avoid losses, betting companies are incentivized to make predictions as accurate as possible (Forrest et al., 2005). With large sums of money at stake, the monetary incentive to predict well is much stronger than in the described traditional forecasting instruments, but should also be stronger than in PMs with no money at stake in play-money markets and little money at stake in real-money markets.

In the field of sports forecasting, we study the forecasting accuracy for predicting the outcomes of soccer matches during the FIFA World Cup 2006. The forecast accuracy of a play-money market where traders could not suffer any losses is compared to two professionally operated fixed odds betting markets. Additionally, we examine whether the PMs outperform a random predictor as well as forecasts that are based on historic data about the success of national soccer teams.

The remainder of the paper is structured as follows: In the next section, we present work related to the analysis of the forecasting accuracy of PMs in general and related work about the efficiency of betting markets. Section 3 describes the event to be analyzed, namely the FIFA World Cup 2006, as well as the design of the STOCCER PM platform including its markets and descriptive statistics about participation in the markets. Also, the analyzed betting markets and the other two benchmarks are outlined. In section 4, the results with respect to the comparison of the forecast accuracy are presented and discussed. Section 5 summarizes the main results.

2. Related Work

2.1. Prediction Markets

Information aggregation with PMs does not have a long tradition in economic research. Starting with the 1988 U.S. presidential election market, the focus of the research field was mainly to study the accuracy of predictions derived from the trading activity within these markets. Political stock markets outperformed election polls in many cases as, for example, many results from the Iowa Electronic Market demonstrate (Berg et al., 2001, Forsythe et al., 1994). Moreover, research in the business forecasting area suggests that PMs can perform better than traditional methods such as business meetings (Sunstein, 2006). Chen and Plott (2002) show that PMs on sales forecasting were significantly better than official company forecasts in 6 out of 8 cases. Over the last three years, the Hollywood Stock Exchange almost perfectly predicted the Oscar award winners (Lamare, 2007) and has beaten the individual and average forecasts of five experts (Pennock et al., 2001). Spann and Skiera (2003) found that, regarding the hit rate, where a "hit" is present when a forecasting instrument has the lowest mean absolute percentage error of all instruments, the Hollywood Stock Exchange is superior to two analyzed experts.

During the last decade, PMs were also employed in the field of sports forecasting. For instance, Servan-Schreiber et al. (Servan-Schreiber et al., 2004) compare the performance of play-money versus real-money PMs and find no significant difference in the forecast accuracy. Moreover, both market types outperformed individual forecasts. However, the markets were very likely not completely identical with regard to number of traders, trading activity or trading fees, which might have played a role in the formation of the prediction (for a discussion see Luckner and Weinhardt (2007)). Regarding the comparison of play- versus real-money markets, Rosenbloom and Notz (2006) find that real-money markets performed better than play-money markets in case of non sports events.

In a paper which deals with the comparisons of PMs and fixed odds betting, Schmidt and Werwatz (2002) analyze a 2000 European Championship market to detect whether a PM is a better predictor in terms of forecasting accuracy than a random predictor. As a second benchmark they use betting odds for the same event from several betting companies. The random predictor performed worse than the markets' predictions. Also, relative to the PMs expert bookmakers forecasted less accurately. One of the key features of these market was the real-money investment which was required; every participant had to deposit a certain amount of money (up to 50€) and thus could suffer losses. As such, these analyzed markets were similar to the ones of the Iowa Electronic Markets, which were shown to be very accurate in the past. However, these markets differ fundamentally from the play-money market STOCCER since our market did not require any real-money investment. Participants could therefore neither lose nor win any money by revealing their expectations.

In a very recent study, Spann and Skiera (2009) analyze the forecast accuracy of a play-money market in comparison to betting odds and tipsters. Their results show that PMs slightly outperform betting odds, while both instruments strongly outperform tipsters. In the study presented in this paper, we also examine different market designs, take historical data into account and provide descriptive statistics about the trading actions in the analyzed markets.

2.2. Fixed Odds Betting

In fixed odds betting, usually one or several professional experts of a company set odds which are usually not, or rarely, adjusted over time (e.g., Forrest et al., 2005). Bettors then accept or reject those bets at some time before the beginning of the decisive event. Essentially, in fixed odds betting, outside information from potentially knowledgeable bettors is not accounted for in the odds. Studies have mostly shown that fixed odds betting markets are efficient (Gandar et al., 1998, Pope and Peel, 1989). For instance, Pope and Peel (1989) develop a linear probability model which incorporates the probabilities of the actual occurrences of the outcomes and the probabilities implicitly quoted by the odd setters, deriving betting strategies and showing that no strategy could lead to expected positive returns.

However, some inefficiencies such as the favorite longshot bias (Cain et al., 2000) were also detected, where favorites are undervalued and "long shots", i.e. subjects with a very low probability of winning, are overvalued.

Forrest et al. (2005) give the main reason why especially in fixed odds betting markets efficiency is required: *"If bets are mispriced, the financial consequences for bookmakers may be serious (...)"*. Although a commission fee of 15-25% is usually charged (Woodland and Woodland, 1994) which can palliate possible losses in the short run, under competition, betting companies setting the odds in consequence have a strong incentive to generate efficient, and therewith accurate, quotes.

3. Data Sets

In this section we firstly describe the event we studied, namely the FIFA World Cup 2006. Secondly, we present the data sources used to forecast the outcome of the World Cup. This includes our PM STOCCER as well as sports betting odds and the FIFA world ranking. Additionally, we also employed a random predictor.

3.1. The FIFA World Cup 2006

The 2006 FIFA World Cup hosted 32 participating national soccer teams from June 9th to July 9th 2006. The preliminary rounds included eight groups with four teams each. The top two teams in each group advanced to the final rounds starting with the round of 16. The final rounds applied a sudden death system until the final game. Additionally, one game was played for the third place between the losers of the two semi final games. In total, 64 matches were played during the tournament, of which 48 matches were played in the preliminary rounds and another 16 in the final rounds.

In the final rounds, matches that were tie after the official 90 minute match time were followed by an overtime period and, if necessary, by a penalty shootout to determine the team qualifying for the next round. In our prognosis data we count ties after the official 90 minute match time as "draw". We did not consider overtimes and penalty shootouts because we regarded their outcomes as more or less unpredictable. This interpretation also holds for the betting odds, where a draw was counted the same way.

3.2. The STOCCER Exchange

In order to study the prediction accuracy of sports PMs, we ran an exchange during the FIFA World Cup 2006. More than 1.500 traders registered for our experimental markets called STOCCER[14]. The web trading interface we provided is depicted in Figure 1. Our exchange started on May 15th 2006 and ran until the end of the FIFA World Cup on July 9th 2006. The trading platform was open to the public 24 hours a day, 7 days a week. On average, more than 1,600 market transactions were executed per day.

Figure 1: Trading screen of STOCCER.

STOCCER hosted two types of markets:

In the championship market, virtual stocks for all the 32 national teams taking part in the FIFA World Cup 2006 were traded. The payoff of the virtual stocks was valued at 50 virtual currency units for the world champion and at 30 virtual currency units for the vice

---

[14] www.stoccer.com

world champion. Table 1 shows the payoff values for teams reaching the semi finals, quarter finals and the round of 16. In case a team did not reach the round of 16 the team's virtual stocks rendered worthless at the end of the tournament.

In the match markets for the final rounds, we traded three stocks for each of the 16 matches – one for every possible outcome of the matches: either team A wins or team B wins or the match is drawn after the second half. The virtual stock corresponding to the event that actually occurred at the end of a match was valued at 10 virtual currency units; the other two assets were worthless.

Type	Number of virtual stocks	Final payoff	Start	End
Championship	1 per country (32)	World champion: 50 Vice WC: 30 Semi finals: 20 Quarter finals: 10 Round of 16: 5 Otherwise: 0	May 15th 2006	July 9th 2006
Match	3 per match: team A wins, team B wins, tie after 2nd half	Event occurred: 10 Otherwise: 0	2 days before the matches	At the end of the matches

Table 1: STOCCER's markets operated during the FIFA World Cup 2006.

Concerning the financial market design these markets used a continuous double auction (CDA) in combination with limit orders. In order to issue shares we decided to make use of so called unit portfolios (see Berg and Rietz, 2003). A portfolio contains one piece of share of every virtual stock which is traded in the respective market. The portfolio price equals the sum of the payoffs for one share of every virtual stock in a market and was, e.g., 10 virtual currency units in the match markets. It thus corresponded to the redemption value for correctly predicting the outcome of a match. Buying and selling of portfolios from and to the market operators is therefore risk free for traders and was possible at all times.

STOCCER operated as a play-money market and provided participants an initial endowment of 100,000 virtual currency units as well as 100 units of every virtual stock. The only extrinsic incentives for traders to join the market and reveal their expectations were a ranking of their user names on the main website and a lottery of prizes. The overall Top 100 traders with the highest deposit value after the end of the tournament took part in a final lottery, where the first prizes were shares of an investment fund with a value of 3,000, 2,000, and 1,000 Euros. Although the total sum of 6,000€ seems quite large at first sight it has to be considered that the probability of winning one of the prizes was quite low, taking into account the more than 1,500 traders. In addition, we weekly raffled an iPod among the 20 most active traders of the preceding week. However, we assume that a large proportion of traders were not only driven by financial rewards but also by their enthusiasm and interest in soccer.

3.3. Sports Betting Odds

As a benchmark for the PM we use the betting odds of two major German sports betting providers: Oddset and Wetten.de. Oddset[15] is Germany's largest betting institution and is owned and controlled by the state. Wetten.de[16] is a popular sports betting provider that is privately held.

Both bookmakers offered fixed odds which bettors could wager against. The fixed odds were set by the bookmaker at the time the odds were placed. For each of the 64 World Cup matches, bets could be placed on a win for the first team (1), a draw (0), and a win for the second team (2). All bets are referring to the score after the official time of 90 minutes. Betting quotes are stated in decimal odds – a bet quoted with 3.5 pays out 3.5 times the wagering amount deployed. A typical betting screen is illustrated in Figure 2. As bookmakers follow a commercial interest and try their best to avoid short term losses (see section 3.3), the odds include a commission fee. This means that wagering the same amount on all three possible outcomes would lead to a 15-25% loss.

The total sales of Oddset in 2006 were 342.3 million Euros. Although we do not have disaggregated data on single categories, with the main sport in Germany being soccer and the main soccer event in 2006 being the FIFA World Championship, we guess that a considerably large amount of money has been betted on these markets for the World Cup.

---

[15] www.oddset.de
[16] www.wetten.de (international site also available at www.digibet.com)

Figure 2: Typical screen of a fixed odds betting site

3.4. FIFA World Ranking

We use the FIFA world ranking[17] as another benchmark which is based on historic data only. The FIFA world ranking from May 2006 is built on a history of the last eight years and takes into account the following factors: outcome of matches, importance of matches, strength of opponents, regional strength, home and away matches, as well as number of matches and goals. For the index, all international "A" matches are relevant. For each individual factor, points are assigned which are then aggregated to an index value. For most factors, complex calculations are used to determine the team's actual state and strength.

3.5. Random Predictor

Forecasts are worthless if they do not result in better predictions than randomly drawing one of the possible outcomes. Thus, we use a random predictor as benchmark to evaluate the forecast accuracy of our PM. As we can observe three possible outcomes for each individual match, an uninformed, random guess would result in a hit rate of 33.33% (for details see Schmidt and Werwatz, 2002).

4. Evaluation of the Forecast Accuracy

PM prices and thus the forecasts of PMs are driven by the information and the expectations of the users trading in the markets (Spann and Skiera, 2003). Beside historic data,

---
[17] www.fifa.com/worldfootball/ranking/

traders also consider current information that is available to them as well as ongoing developments during the tournament and even during matches.

To compare the forecasting accuracy of our markets to predictions derived from the random predictor, the FIFA ranking and the betting odds, we calculate the hit rate, i.e. the percentage of correctly predicted games, for each forecasting instrument. In Table 2, we compare the hit rate of the different instruments for the whole sample of 64 matches.

In case of the STOCCER championship market, we predict a win for the team with the higher stock price prior to the kick off of the match. We predict a draw whenever the stock prices of two teams are equal. For the betting odds, we consider the outcome with the lowest odds as the prediction. In case of the FIFA ranking we predict a win for the team that has the better position in the ranking.

Instrument	No. obs.	Hit rate	% improvement[18]	p-value[19]
Championship market	64	59.38%		
Oddset odds	64	57.81%	2.72%	0.799
Wetten.de odds	64	67.19%	-11.62%	0.203
FIFA ranking	64	46.88%	26.66%	0.042
Random draw	64	33.33%	78.14%	< 0.001

Table 2: Comparison of forecast accuracy (all matches)

When comparing the hit rates of the championship market, the betting odds, the FIFA ranking and the random predictor for all 64 matches, we find that championship market indeed yields a higher hit rate than the FIFA ranking and the random draw model. The difference in the hit rate of the PM and the two other instruments is significant in both cases (p < 0.05). The forecasts can be improved when using a PM instead of these two instruments. Table 2 shows the percentage of improvement when one replaces the respective alternative instrument with a PM. When comparing the championship market with the two sports betting odds, we find the Stoccer championship market to outperform Oddset on the one hand, while Wetten.de is superior to the Stoccer championship market on the other hand. In both cases, however, the difference in the hit rate is not significant. This can be considered as a clear success for the PM because the forecast accuracy is similar as in case of betting odds, even though the market was a play-money market and the likelihood of draws is underesti-

---
[18] Percentage of improvement of championship market over alternative instrument
[19] Chi-square test for difference to hit rate of championship market

mated in the championship market. Based on market prices in the championship market we would only predict a draw if the prices were exactly the same – which is rather unlikely. This also hold for the FIFA ranking where we would predict a draw if two teams were ranked equally.

As described in section 3.2, we also operated separate markets for the 16 matches in the final rounds. To calculate the hit rate in case of the match markets we predict the outcome with the highest stock price out of the three possible outcomes of a match. We compare the forecasts of these 16 match markets to the forecasts of the other instruments. The results of this comparison are shown in Table 3.

Instrument	No. Obs.	Hit rate	% improvement[20]	p-value[21]
Match market	16	62.50%		
Championship market	16	43.75%	42.86%	0.121
Oddset odds	16	43.75%	42.86%	0.121
Wetten.de odds	16	43.75%	42.86%	0.121
FIFA ranking	16	25.00%	150.00%	0.002
Random draw	16	33.33%	87.52%	0.010

Table 3: Comparison of forecast accuracy (final rounds).

For the last 16 matches of the tournament, the hit rate of the match markets is again significantly higher than the hit rate of the FIFA ranking and of the random draw model. Interestingly, the hit rate is higher in case of the match markets than it is when predicting a win for the team with the higher stock price in the championship market. One reason for this insignificant difference could again be the fact that the likelihood of draws is underestimated in the championship market. Furthermore, traders in match markets can focus on the outcome of one match at a time instead of trying to predict the course of the entire tournament. In the final rounds, the match markets also outperform predictions based on the championship market as well as the betting odds – although the difference is not statistically significant. Moreover, the forecast accuracy of the championship market is the same as the forecast accuracy of the betting odds.

---

[20] Percentage of improvement of match market over alternative instrument
[21] Chi-square test for difference to hit rate of match market

At first sight, it is somewhat surprising that the hit rate for the championship market, the betting odds and the FIFA ranking is on average lower for the last 16 matches than it is when taking into account all 64 matches. However, we think this is plausible since it should be easier to predict the outcome of matches at the beginning of the tournament than at the end. At the beginning, there are numerous underdogs and clear favorites whereas the performance of teams will not differ that much at the end of the tournament. Thus, it is presumably much harder to predict the outcome of matches taking place in the last rounds compared to earlier matches.

5. Summary

In this paper, we presented and analyzed a sports PM we were running during the FIFA World Cup 2006. The goal of our paper was to study the forecasting accuracy of a play-money PM where traders could not suffer any losses compared to forecasts that are based on odds which were set by professional bookmakers. These bookmakers' odds are strongly incentivized to give predictions as accurate as possible due to the high monetary investments that are at stake. We could not find any statistically significant difference in the forecasts with respect to hit rates. Both methods provide a comparable forecasting accuracy. As another benchmark, we used the FIFA world ranking for our study, which is calculated based on the historic performance of the national soccer teams. We could observe a significantly better forecasting accuracy for our PMs as well as betting odds. Moreover, the random predictor is clearly inferior to the forecasts of our PMs.

By demonstrating the competitiveness of play-money PMs compared to sports betting forecasts, our results align with those attained by Schmidt and Werwatz (2002). However, the markets in their research used real money as an incentive and participants hence were directly punished financially in case of a poor forecasting performance. Play-money PMs as the one we analyzed in this paper, however, are much easier to set up and to operate than real-money PMs due to legal and technical reasons, which also facilitates the development of corresponding IS platforms. In the research line of play-money markets, our results align with the work of Spann and Skiera (2009).

When keeping in mind that betting odds have shown to be extremely good predictors and that similar instruments are mostly non existent in other fields of application beyond sports forecasting, real-money as well as play-money PMs indeed seem to be a very promising forecasting instrument.

References

Berg, J. E., Forsythe, R., Nelson, F. & Rietz, T. A. (2001) Results from a Dozen Years of Election Futures Markets Research. In Plott, C. & Smith, V. L. (Eds.) *Handbook of Experimental Economic Results.*

Berg, J. E. & Rietz, T. A. (2003) Prediction Markets as Decision Support Systems. *Information Systems Frontiers,* 5 (1), 79-93.

Cain, M., Law, D. & Peel, D. (2000) The Favourite-Longshot Bias and Market Efficiency in UK Football betting. *Scottish Journal of Political Economy,* 47 (1), 25-36.

Chen, K.-Y. & Plott, C. R. (2002) Information Aggregation Mechanisms: Concept, Design and Implementation for a Sales Forecasting Problem. *Social Science Working Paper No.1131, California Institute of Technology.*

Elberse, A. (2007) The Power of Stars: Do Star Actors Drive the Success of Movies? *Journal of Marketing,* 71 (4), 102-120.

Fama, E. F. (1970) Efficient capital markets: A Review of Theory and Empirical Work. *Journal of Finance,* 25 (2), 383-417.

Fama, E. F. (1991) Efficient Capital Markets: II. *Journal of Finance,* 46 (5), 1575-1617.

Forrest, D., Goddard, J. & Simmons, R. (2005) Odds-Setters as Forecasters: The Case of English Football. *International Journal of Forecasting,* 21 (3), 551-564.

Forsythe, R., Frank, M., Krishnamurthy, V. & Ross, T. W. (1995) Using Market Prices to Predict Election Results: The 1993 UBC Election Stock Market. *The Canadian Journal of Economics* 28 (4), 770-793.

Forsythe, R., Nelson, F., Neumann, G. & Wright, J. (1994) The 1992 Iowa Political Stock Market: September Forecasts. *The Political Methodologist,* 5 (2), 15-19.

Gandar, J. M., Dare, W. H., Brown, C. R. & Zuber, R. A. (1998) Informed Traders and Price Variations in the Betting Market for Professional Basketball Games. *The Journal of Finance,* 53 (1), 385-401.

Glosten, L. R. & Milgrom, P. R. (1985) Bid, Ask and Transaction Prices in a Specialist Market With Heterogeneously Informed Traders. *Journal of Financial Economics,* 14 (1), 71-100.

Hayek, F. (1945) The Use of Knowledge in Society. *American Economic Review,* 35 (4), 519-530.

Kiviat, B. (2004) The End of Management? *TIME, Inside Business.* July 12.

Lamare, A. (2007) Hollywood Stock Exchange (HSX.com) Traders correctly picked 7 out of 8 Top Category Oscar Winners to continue its stellar record. *Available at http://www.hsx.com/about/press/070226.htm.*

Luckner, S. & Weinhardt, C. (2007) How to Pay Traders in Information Markets? Results from a Field Experiment. *Journal of Prediction Markets,* 1 (2), 147-156.

Ortner, G. (1997) Forecasting Markets - An Industrial Application: Part I. *Working Paper, TU Vienna.*

Pennock, D. M., Lawrence, S., Nielsen, F. A. & Giles, C. L. (2001) The Real Power of Artificial Markets. *Science,* 291, 987-988.

Plott, C. R. (2000) Markets as Information Gathering Tools. *Southern Economic Journal,* 67 (1), 1-15.

Pope, P. F. & Peel, D. A. (1989) Information, Prices and Efficiency in a Fixed-Odds Betting Market. *Economica,* 56 (223), 323-341.

Rosenbloom, E. S. & Notz, W. W. (2006) Statistical Tests of Real-Money versus Play-Money Prediction Markets. *Electronic Markets,* 16 (1), 63-69.

Schmidt, C. & Werwatz, A. (2002) How Well do Markets Predict the Outcome of an Event? The Euro 2000 Soccer Championships Experiment. *Discussion Papers on Strategic Interaction Jena, Germany, Max Planck Institute for Research into Economic Systems.*

Servan-Schreiber, E., Wolfers, J., Pennock, D. & Galebach, B. (2004) Prediction Markets: Does Money Matter? *Electronic Markets,* 14 (3), 243-251.

Slamka, C., Soukhoroukova, A. & Spann, M. (2008) Event Studies in Play- and Real Money Prediction Market. *Journal of Prediction Markets,* 2 (2), 53-70.

Soukhoroukova, A. & Spann, M. (2005) New Product Development with Internet-based Information Markets: Theory and Empirical Application. *13th European Conference on Information Systems (ECIS).*

Spann, M. & Skiera, B. (2003) Internet-Based Virtual Stock Markets for Business Forecasting. *Management Science,* 49 (10), 1310-1326.

Spann, M. & Skiera, B. (2009) Sports Forecasting: A Comparison of the Forecast Accuracy of Prediction Markets, Betting Odds and Tipsters. *Journal of Forecasting,* 28 (1), 55-77.

Sunstein, C. R. (2006) Deliberation and Information Markets. In Hahn, W. & Tetlock, P. C. (Eds.) *Information Markets: A New Way of Making Decisions.* Washington D.C., AEI-Brookings Press.

Woodland, L. M. & Woodland, B. M. (1994) Market Efficiency and the Favorite-Longshot Bias: The Baseball Betting Market. *The Journal of Finance,* 49 (1), 269-279.

Event Studies in Real- and Play-Money Prediction Markets

Christian Slamka[1], Arina Soukhoroukova, Martin Spann[2]

[1] School of Business and Economics, Goethe-University Frankfurt, Germany
[2] Chair of Marketing and Innovation, University of Passau, Germany

Abstract

Event study methodology is a powerful procedure to quantify the impact of events and managerial decisions such as new product announcements on the value of a publicly traded company. However, for many events, appropriate financial data may not be available, either because suitable securities are not traded on financial markets or confounding effects limit the insights from financial data. In such instances, prediction markets could potentially provide the necessary data for an event study. Prediction markets are electronic markets where participants can trade stocks whose prices reflect the outcome of future events, e.g. election outcomes, sports results, new product sales or internal project deadlines. One key distinction between different prediction market applications is whether they require real money investments or play-money investment with non monetary incentives for traders.

Thus, the goal of this paper is to compare prediction markets' ability to conduct event studies with respect to these two different incentive schemes. We empirically test the applicability of event study methodology in real-money vs. play-money prediction markets with two data sets. We show that event studies with prediction markets deliver robust and valid results with both incentive schemes.

Keywords: prediction markets, event evaluation, decision making, event studies, play money vs. real money

1. Introduction

On the day of the iPhone announcement, the stock price of Apple soared 7% in 2006, while the stock of its competitor Research in Motion, the producer of Blackberry, slumped 6%. With such milestone events for publicly traded companies, the public assessment on managerial decisions is clearly reflected in the subsequent market reaction. One common approach to assess the impact of an event is to extract the very reaction caused by the event on the company's stock return. Analyzing stock market reactions helps to quantify the financial impact of company specific or market wide events on the company's market capitalization (MacKinlay, 1997). Such information can provide a valuable retrospective assessment of managerial actions and serve as a prospective estimation for similar future events.

The basic idea behind market based evaluation of events is that the prices on a competitive market efficiently aggregate all (public) information available to the market participants (Fama, 1970). Market efficiency implies that new information is subsequently incorporated in market returns, making the (financial) impact of that information quantifiable. Today, the so called event study methodology is widely accepted as a standard procedure to measure the impact of events with more than 500 papers published in leading journals since the 1970s (Kothari and Warner, 2006). Examples of applications include the impact of new product introductions (c.f. Chaney et al., 1991), the timing of stock options awards to CEOs (Yermack, 1997), mergers of firms (Rosen, 2006) or even changes of a company's name (Horsky and Swyngedouw, 1987).

In general, for the application of this rather clear cut procedure, an appropriate security must be traded on an efficient financial market and the event must have a significant impact on the company's performance in order to induce a measurable effect on its stock returns. In cases where these prerequisites are not met, prediction markets (PMs), also referred to as virtual stock markets or information markets, can provide the required market data for such an analysis. PMs can model nearly any future forecasting goal as a virtual stock as long as its final date and its final outcome can be quantified (Spann and Skiera, 2003). The forecasting goal of a virtual stock is very adaptable: it can refer to a vote share of a party or market share of a product, product units sold or success probabilities of different projects. Today, various PMs operate to predict the outcomes of political, financial, sports or movie related events, ranging from small scale markets with as few as a dozen participants (Christiansen, 2007) to more than one hundred thousand, as for example on the Hollywood Stock Exchange. Moreover, PMs can generally be relatively easily implemented. In business environments, various companies such as Google, Yahoo!, General Electric, Microsoft, Qualcomm or Eli Lilly have already applied company internal PMs (e.g., Chen and Plott, 2002, Ostrover, 2005).

Although PMs employ the same market based mechanism for information aggregation as financial markets, PMs differ from financial markets in several aspects concerning the stock price definition and stock's lifetime, and the amount of financial investment being traded (real vs. play money). The use of play-money vs. real-money as investment scheme in PMs has been debated with respect to participants' trading strategies (Gruca et al., 2003), incentives (Luckner and Weinhardt, 2007) and forecasting accuracy (Servan-Schreiber et al., 2004). Real-money markets have closest resemblance to financial markets with the facet of real money being at stake. Moreover, different types of potentially less informed traders might participate in play-money markets. However, legal restrictions which prohibit the use of real-money markets and which exist for example in the United States may be an insuperable barrier for the use of real-money markets in certain circumstances. Therefore, when setting up markets with the aim of extending the PMs' field of application by using event study methodology, one key question is whether play-money suffices in general and if there are differences to real-money markets.

Thus, the objective of this paper is to test the applicability of the event study methodology for PMs with different investment schemes. We empirically test the performance of event study methodology in real- vs. play-money PMs based on two data sets of PMs for the same set of events using four evaluation criteria.

The remainder of the paper is organized as follows: Section 2 covers the basic idea and previous research on PMs. Section 3 describes the data and the event study design used for the analyses. The evaluation criteria and results are outlined in section 4. The general discussion in section 5 summarizes the findings and discusses areas of future research.

2. Prediction Markets

2.1. Idea and Theoretical Foundations of Prediction Markets

In PMs, outcomes of future events are modeled as virtual stocks, whilst the underlying payoff function determines the stocks' (terminal) values after a certain date. As on financial markets, a trader will sell an overvalued stock and buy an undervalued stock, according to his or her assessment of the stock's fair value and its comparison to the current market price. The assessment of the future value is dependent on the traders' opinions of the outcome of the stock's underlying event. Consequently, the price of a virtual stock reflects the aggregate expectations of all participants in case of an efficient market (Wolfers and Zitzewitz, 2006). Thus, PMs can be used to derive predictions on the respective outcomes (Manski, 2006). In almost two decades of research, the forecasts of PMs have been found to be generally at least as accurate compared to alternatives such as opinion polls or expert surveys (e.g., Forsythe et al., 1999, Spann and Skiera, 2003).

In a PM, the remuneration of a participant is positively dependent on his predictive and trading performance, that is, his deposit value after the payoff is determined based on the outcome of the events. Therefore, the results of a PM might be less biased towards personal preferences as the participants seek to maximize their deposit values (e.g., Spann and Skiera, 2003). And, even though the majority of traders might be prone to make mistakes, a small group of "knowledgeable" participants will exploit such inefficiencies and set efficient prices (Forsythe et al., 1999, Oliven and Rietz, 2004). Some PMs require rather small (such as the Iowa Electronic Markets) or even permit significant (the first PM in this study) real-money investments, but also play-money markets as the Hollywood Stock Exchange, NewsFutures and IdeaFutures have independently shown to perform well, regarding point predictions on specific dates (Pennock et al., 2000, Servan-Schreiber et al., 2004, Spann and Skiera, 2003).

A great scope of versatile design options concerning forecasting goal, different number of participants, and market structures exist among various PMs. In general, the design of a PM has to be carefully calibrated to the type of forecasting goal and the setting of the market (e.g., Spann and Skiera, 2003).

One of the main design options is the choice of the payoff function. Generally, the (terminal) value (payoff) of a virtual stock after a certain event date T, that is, the (play-)

money each stock owner receives after the event occurs, is dependent on the true value of the outcome that is transferred via the payoff function ϕ:

(1) $$d_i = \phi(Z_i), \ i \in I,$$

where

d_i = payoff of virtual stock i,

$\phi(\cdot)$ = payoff function,

Z_i = actual outcome of stock i's forecasting goal at time T, and

I = index set of stocks.

Other design options are the market mechanism, different incentive schemes (Luckner and Weinhardt, 2007) and the duration of the PM. For respective taxonomies see Spann and Skiera (2003) and Wolfers and Zitzewitz (2004).

3. Previous Research on Continuous Reactions of Prediction Market Prices to Events and Comparisons of Play- and Real-Money Markets

The majority of previous research focuses on the forecast accuracy of PMs compared with alternative forecasting methods at one specific point in time, i.e., the final prediction, rather than on the development of prices over time. For a detailed overview of the current research and studies see Tziralis and Tatsiopoulos (2007).

Few studies analyze the continuous reactions of prices on PMs to events: Berg and Rietz (2003) propose to use PMs along with conditional PMs as decision support systems by analyzing the correlation of different stocks over time. Pennock et al. (2002) develop a model of how new information is incorporated into market prices and test an algorithm for automatically detecting and explaining events with external datasources such as Usenet. Wolfers and Zitzewitz (2009) and Snowberg et al. (2007) extract additional, otherwise "oblique", information from financial markets data with the help of PMs. They suggest that PMs can help to understand the movements of financial markets by incorporating ex ante expectations and as a result, for example, being able to quantify the monetary value of political actions or major events during an election.

Elberse (2007) conducts a classic event study procedure with the data provided by Hollywood Stock Exchange on a daily data basis. Borghesi (2006) applies the event study methodology with minute wise data to analyze a real-money market where he detects that market participants underreact to new information. In a recent study, Easton and Uylangco (2007) analyze a real-money cricket betting market and find rapid information incorporation as a result of news and a high predictive validity of odds. However, the investigated market is not a virtual stock market as such, where stocks can be bought and sold, but relies on odds which traders set.

No study that we are aware of has compared the performance of real-money markets and play-money markets concerning continuous reaction to events. One of the two known studies to date which compare play-money market with real-money markets focuses on forecast accuracy with an analysis of NFL (American football league) game markets and finds no significant difference between the forecast accuracy of either market (Servan-Schreiber et al., 2004). Rosenbloom and Notz (2006) find that in non sports events, real-money markets are more accurate than play-money markets. However, for sports events, they are comparably accurate. Additionally, a new study (Luckner and Weinhardt, 2007) has compared the effect of different incentive schemes on the predictive accuracy of PMs, where the authors show that, surprisingly, a rank order tournament leads to better prediction results than a performance related incentive scheme.

4. Goal and Design of Empirical Study

4.1. Goal of the Study

The analysis of previous research on PMs revealed that the applicability of the event study methodology in PMs with real-money vs. play-money investments has not been compared yet. However, this design consideration may be critical for the ability of a PM to provide data for event studies, especially for short horizon events. Therefore, we want to test the performance of the event study methodology in PMs with both investment schemes.

4.2. Data and Requirements

For the goal of our study, we choose a data set which includes two PMs (play and real money) for the same set of events. Further, this data set had to include a sufficient number of events for our analysis. Finally and most importantly, the data should meet the requirements for the application of event study methodology (McWilliams and Siegel, 1997):

(a) The market is (semi strong) efficient with all publicly available information being reflected in the stock prices.
(b) No confounding effects which might have an influence on stock returns occur in the estimation or event windows.
(c) Events must be unanticipated since otherwise, they are already incorporated in stock returns in case of market efficiency.

We choose to use data from two major sports PMs conducted during the 2004 European soccer championship. The European soccer tournament lasted three weeks in June 2004 with 16 teams playing 31 games. The first three games for each team were played in group games (overall 4 groups) to qualify for the quarter finals, where the knock out rounds started. The event study is conducted during the games, which is the time period when the major events occur.

For the requirements of an event study, we conclude that the existence of market efficiency (a) cannot be determined prior to conducting the event study. However, the market data and events to be analyzed can be selected in advance according to requirements (b) and (c). In this case, sports (soccer) market data serves as ideal basis for this research and has been used in a number of previous studies (e.g., Rosenbloom and Notz, 2006, Luckner and Weinhardt, 2007, Servan-Schreiber et al., 2004). First, during soccer games, no confounding effects exist that could add unwanted noise (requirement (b)). Events which are subject to possible confounding effect can be excluded from the study if all relevant event data is present (which is the case for our data sets). Then, because of fast actions and sudden incidences in soccer games, events can hardly be anticipated (requirement (c)). Moreover, as a consequence of the decisive events clustered in ninety minutes of the game, the trading volume during the game is exceedingly high compared to non playing time, allowing for a fine grained intra game analysis.

4.3. Prediction Market Design

Both PMs were operated and developed by professional firms. The real-money PM1 was operated by a major German betting company for sport and finance related events. The play-money PM2 was conducted as an online competition for a major online broker, also offered by a firm specialized in online games and contests. Both web based user interfaces offered rich information on the teams, the stock history and the respective events, as well as dynamic price charts and the best five open bid and ask orders. Both PMs' employed a continuous double auction as market mechanism, which is the common mechanism used in financial markets. See Table 1 for an overview of the two PMs.

	PM1	PM2
Forecasting goal	outcome of one game	final standing of a team in the tournament
Investment type	real money investment	play money
Initial endowment	no initial endowment	100 stocks per team + 30,000 monetary units
No. of markets	31 (one per game)	1 (during tournament)
No. of stocks	3 per game (Team A wins / Team B wins / draw after the regular playing time)	16 (one for each team)
Payoff function	winner takes all	multi part step
Trading mechanism	continuous double auction	continuous double auction
No. of registered traders	6,569	9,077

Table 1: Overview of prediction markets in data sets

4.3.1 Prediction market 1 (PM1): real-money market

In PM1 three kinds of winner takes all stocks existed for each game: two for the cases team A or team B wins, and one if there was a draw, which was defined as the case when the scores were equal after the regular playing time. The winning stock was valued at 10€, the remaining two stocks at 0 €:

$$(2) \quad d_{i,A/B/Draw}^{PM1} = \begin{cases} 10 \text{ €, if Team A wins / Team B wins / Draw in i-th game,} \\ 0 \text{ €, otherwise.} \end{cases}$$

Thus, the price of a virtual stock at a given point in time (divided by 10) can be interpreted as the likelihood for the corresponding event to occur (Wolfers and Zitzewitz 2006). The participants could trade virtual stocks as long as they had a sufficient amount of money in their cash deposit to buy (no short positions were allowed) or sufficient stocks in their portfolio to sell. In addition, the provider charged a 2% commission fee for each trade.

4.3.2 Prediction market 2 (PM2): play-money market

In PM2, the goal was to predict the final standings of the team, which was reflected in the multi part payoff function (MU: monetary units) of virtual currency that did not correspond to any real world currency:

$$(3) \quad d_i^{PM2} = \begin{cases} 300 \text{ MU, if team } i \text{ becomes champion,} \\ 200 \text{ MU, if team } i \text{ becomes vice-champion,} \\ 150 \text{ MU, if team } i \text{ is eliminated in the semi-finals,} \\ 100 \text{ MU, if team } i \text{ is eliminated in the quarter finals,} \\ 75 \text{ MU, if team } i \text{ becomes third in group games,} \\ 50 \text{ MU, if team } i \text{ becomes fourth in group games.} \end{cases}, \text{ with } i \in \{1,...,16\}.$$

The traders were incentivized by the possibility to win prizes, which were given to top performers.

4.4. Event Study Design

4.4.1 Event data collection

The data on events was retrieved from the official UEFA (Union of European Soccer Associations) database. In total, over 400 events were collected, including minor events as yellow cards or player substitutions. The exact times have additionally been double checked with minute by minute game descriptions of three data sources: the major German sports newspaper "Kicker", the German sports internet portal "Sport1", and the "BBC" online sports section. We only take goals into consideration since they have the most decisive impact on the game and tournament outcomes and thus on stock returns compared to other events such as yellow/red cards or player substitutions.

Moreover, we focus on the total set of 77 goals. Goals from penalty shots were excluded since the penalty shots' outcomes could be anticipated with the referee decision (violating the 3rd prerequisite). For example, 75 % of penalty shots are turned into goals in Italian and French soccer (Chiappori et al., 2002). Additionally, goals in overtime were excluded because PM1 predicted only the outcome after the regular playing time. We set the estimation and event period to 7 and 4 minutes, respectively, based on the tradeoff between availability of data for model estimation and availability of events. To avoid confounding events, we omitted those goals which were preceded by events (including events with low impact such as yellow cards) during the estimation period or which were succeeded by other events during the event period. In addition, the events in concurrent games of the same group in the last games of the preliminary round were also excluded. Moreover, trading data was not present for a few sections of games, apparently due to server downtime. This leaves a total of 42 goals to be analyzed for both PM1 and PM2.

4.4.2 Expected Return Model

In event study literature, basically two types of models to determine expected returns exist (for overviews see Binder, 1998, Kothari and Warner, 2006, MacKinlay, 1997, McKenzie et al., 2004). *Non market based models* do not include return correlation with other stocks while *market based models* also consider correlation with other stocks' returns (see the Appendix for the standard procedure of the event study methodology). In financial markets, usually market based models (e.g., Kothari and Warner, 2006) are applied to determine expected returns in the event window in order to account for overall market or index movements non conditional on the particular event affecting only one stock's returns. However, in case of PM1 and PM2 in this study, single stocks' prices, and thus, returns, in a market are negatively correlated. For example, in PM1, a winner takes all payoff function is used, implying that in case of market efficiency, all prices of stocks sum up to a given, predetermined amount. Thus, we have

(4) $$c = \sum_{i \in I} p_{i,t} = p_{j,t} + \sum_{i \in I, i \neq j} p_{i,t} = \underbrace{(p_{j,t} + \delta)}_{p_{j,t+1}} + \underbrace{\left(\sum_{i \in I, i \neq j} p_{i,t} - \delta \right)}_{\sum_{i \in I, i \neq j} p_{i,t+1}} = c,$$

showing the negative correlation of stock prices (and implicitly, stock returns). Ultimately, an appropriate index cannot be created and only non market based models can be applied. A similar rationale applies for PM2. Thus, for both PMs, we use the (non market) constant mean return model (CMR) (MacKinlay, 1997).

We test the significance of the aggregated abnormal returns (AAR) for a certain period t by using the t-statistic from Brown and Warner (1985), which is $\lambda_t^{AAR} = \frac{AAR_t}{SD(\overline{AAR})} \sim N(0,1)$. $SD(\overline{AAR})$ is the standard deviation of the mean of aggregated abnormal returns in the estimation window. We test the significance of the cumulative aggregated abnormal returns (CAARs) with the t-statistic described in Kothari and Warner (2006), which is $\lambda_t^{CAAR} = \frac{CAAR_t}{\sqrt{L * \text{var}(\overline{AAR})}} = \frac{CAAR_t}{\sqrt{L} * SD(\overline{AAR})}$, where $L = |t - t_1 + 1|$.

Although we have a lower number of transactions in PM1 than in PM2 (see Table 1), we choose to set the length of a period t to 20 seconds for both markets since an extension to 30 seconds would not have decreased the number of missing values substantially. For both PMs, we use the last price reported during the period of 20 seconds. In case of missing values in a specific period, the last transaction price is used. In order to achieve an easy interpretability of returns, we compute relative returns instead of log returns.

5. Results of Empirical Study

5.1. Evaluation Criteria

We investigate the applicability of event study methodology for both incentive schemes based on the following criteria, which reflect the degree of market efficiency and the stability of the event study results:

1. *Magnitude and stability of the stock price reaction and stability of returns.* We conduct an event study for all events and stocks with different types of goals and measure the reaction to events which is reflected in the AARs and the CAARs
2. *Speed of information incorporation.* Significant abnormal returns in the event window indicate if new information is incorporated in the market. Therefore, we calculate the number of periods in which the AARs are significant during the event window for each

event and stock independently and quantify how fast the new information is reflected in stock prices. The speed of information incorporation is lower if more periods with significant AARs are observed.

3. *Change of predictive accuracy.* We compute the absolute error (AE) of the predictive accuracy before and after the event to obtain possible improvement rates as a consequence of market reactions to events.

4. *Liquidity.* We compare both PMs with respect to their liquidity by various measures.

5.2. Evaluation Results

5.2.1 Magnitude of stock price reactions and stability of returns

The results of the event study with all 42 events are displayed in Table 2, Table 3 and Figure 1. In PM1, the AARs are significant ($p < 0.01$) from the 100-second to the 60-second period for goals (except in the 40-second period) and remain insignificant thereafter. The highest impact with a high t-value of 29.66 can be observed for the 40-second period. The CAARs remain significant ($p < 0.01$) from the first significant reaction of the AARs on.

For goals against, AARs show a significant reaction ($p < 0.01$) from the 60-second period on, in conjunction with the reaction of the CAARs in this period. The CAARs remain significant, while the AARs become insignificant from the 60-second period on. The difference of the timing of significant periods indicates that participants first trade the stock of the scoring team and subsequently the stocks of the other team. Comparing the magnitude of reactions, goals, with a CAAR of 115.45 at the end of the event window (120-seconds period), have a considerably larger impact than goals against (CAAR = -47.69), meaning that on average goals add 115 % value to the corresponding stock, while goals against take about 48 % off the respective stocks' values . The case for the draw stocks is less clear. As it can be inferred from Figure 1, CAARs first increase and then decrease again. AARs significantly rise in the -100-/-80-/-40-seconds periods and fall in the 0-/40-/80-seconds periods. CAARs are only significant from the -80- until the 100-second period.

sec.	Goal AAR	t		CAAR	t		Goal Against AAR	t		CAAR	t		Draw AAR	t		CAAR	t	
-320	-1.30	-1.58		-1.72	-0.66		-1.00	-0.90		1.36	0.39		0.46	0.85		0.20	0.12	
-300	-0.07	-0.09		-1.81	-0.74		-0.68	-0.62		0.68	0.20		0.10	0.18		0.30	0.18	
-280	1.91	2.33	**	0.52	0.22		1.50	1.35		2.17	0.69		-0.55	-1.00		-0.25	-0.16	
-260	-0.27	-0.33		0.18	0.08		-0.85	-0.76		1.33	0.45		0.30	0.55		0.05	0.04	
-240	0.19	0.24		0.42	0.21		0.96	0.86		2.29	0.84		0.30	0.55		0.35	0.26	
-220	0.00	0.00		0.42	0.23		-0.52	-0.47		1.77	0.71		0.21	0.38		0.56	0.46	
-200	-1.22	-1.49		-1.06	-0.65		-1.35	-1.22		0.42	0.19		0.15	0.28		0.71	0.65	
-180	0.00	0.00		-1.07	-0.75		0.04	0.03		0.45	0.23		-0.33	-0.60		0.38	0.40	
-160	0.41	0.50		-0.57	-0.49		-0.30	-0.27		0.15	0.10		0.43	0.78		0.81	1.05	
-140	-0.21	-0.25		-0.82	-1.00		-0.24	-0.22		-0.09	-0.08		-0.66	-1.20		0.15	0.28	
-120	0.67	0.82		0.00	0.00		0.09	0.08		0.00	0.00		-0.15	-0.28		0.00	0.00	
-100	3.30	4.03	***	4.03	4.91	***	-2.38	-2.14	**	-2.38	-2.14	**	3.18	5.83	***	5.83	10.66	***
-80	12.30	15.01	***	19.04	16.42	***	-1.71	-1.54		-4.09	-2.60	**	4.88	8.92	***	14.75	19.08	***
-60	7.55	9.21	***	28.24	19.89	***	-4.07	-3.67	***	-8.17	-4.24	***	-1.10	-2.01	*	12.74	13.46	***
-40	24.31	29.66	***	57.91	35.32	***	-8.96	-8.06	***	-17.13	-7.71	***	6.30	11.53	***	24.27	22.20	***
-20	18.64	22.74	***	80.64	44.00	***	-11.61	-10.45	***	-28.74	-11.57	***	-0.43	-0.78		23.49	19.22	***
0	11.57	14.11	***	94.75	47.20	***	-16.51	-14.86	***	-45.25	-16.62	***	-4.49	-8.22	***	15.27	11.41	***
20	10.34	12.61	***	107.37	49.51	***	-3.62	-3.26	***	-48.88	-16.62	***	-0.58	-1.06		14.21	9.83	***
40	-1.13	-1.38		105.99	45.72	***	-3.39	-3.05	***	-52.27	-16.63	***	-2.59	-4.74	***	9.47	6.13	***
60	6.14	7.49	***	113.48	46.15	***	-0.30	-0.27		-52.57	-15.77	***	0.22	0.41		9.88	6.03	***
80	0.86	1.05		114.54	44.19	***	2.89	2.60	**	-49.67	-14.13	***	-1.94	-3.55	***	6.33	3.66	***
100	1.21	1.47		116.01	42.68	***	1.53	1.38		-48.14	-13.06	***	-1.47	-2.69	**	3.65	2.01	*
120	-0.46	-0.56		115.45	40.66	***	0.45	0.41		-47.69	-12.39	***	0.21	0.39		4.04	2.13	**

Table 2: (Cumulative) Average Abnormal Returns of PM1
(n.s.: not significant, *: $p < 0.1$, **: $p < 0.05$, ***: $p < 0.01$)

Sec.	Goal				Goal Against			
	AAR	t	CAAR	t	AAR	t	CAAR	t
-320	0.01	0.24	0.09	0.63	-0.06	-0.78	-0.03	-0.11
-300	0.00	-0.06	0.09	0.65	0.02	0.33	-0.08	-0.38
-280	-0.05	-0.98	0.04	0.34	0.12	1.58	-0.06	-0.28
-260	0.00	-0.06	0.04	0.34	0.08	1.05	0.06	0.30
-240	-0.04	-0.85	0.00	0.02	-0.08	-1.14	0.13	0.75
-220	0.04	0.79	0.04	0.38	-0.11	-1.47	0.05	0.31
-200	0.02	0.41	0.06	0.63	0.11	1.53	-0.06	-0.39
-180	0.01	0.26	0.07	0.88	-0.04	-0.48	0.06	0.44
-160	-0.01	-0.11	0.06	1.00	0.02	0.30	0.02	0.20
-140	-0.01	-0.21	0.06	1.20	-0.04	-0.58	0.04	0.58
-120	-0.06	-1.20	0.00	- -	-0.08	-1.05	0.00	- -
-100	-0.06	-1.21	-0.06	-1.21	-0.02	-0.27	-0.08	-1.05
-80	-0.02	-0.39	-0.07	-1.13	0.06	0.82	-0.10	-0.93
-60	0.16	3.48 ***	0.09	1.09	-0.44	-5.98 ***	-0.04	-0.29
-40	0.62	13.51 ***	0.71	7.70 ***	-0.38	-5.23 ***	-0.47	-3.24 ***
-20	0.13	2.94 ***	0.84	8.20 ***	-1.47	-20.04 ***	-0.86	-5.24 ***
0	0.27	5.97 ***	1.12	9.92 ***	-1.65	-22.52 ***	-2.32	-12.96 ***
20	0.92	20.01 ***	2.04	16.75 ***	-0.75	-10.28 ***	-3.97	-20.51 ***
40	0.74	16.13 ***	2.78	21.37 ***	-0.09	-1.22	-4.72	-22.82 ***
60	-0.10	-2.16 **	2.68	19.43 ***	-0.63	-8.68 ***	-4.81	-21.92 ***
80	-0.05	-0.98	2.63	18.12 ***	0.09	1.20	-5.44	-23.54 ***
100	-0.03	-0.69	2.60	17.07 ***	-0.10	-1.31	-5.36	-22.09 ***
120	0.15	3.27 ***	2.75	17.28 ***	0.31	4.28 ***	-5.45	-21.52 ***

Table 3: (Cumulative) Average Abnormal Returns of PM2
(n.s.: not significant, *: p < 0.1, **: p < 0.05, ***: p < 0.01)

In PM2 (Table 3), the first significant reaction in case of goals of the AARs can be observed in the 60-seconds period, staying significant until the 40-seconds period (where p < 0.01). The 120-seconds period has a significant AAR as well, however, the t-values of -3.27 is considerably lower than those of the significant AARs before. The CAARs are consistently significant from the 40-seconds period on.

In case of negative events (i.e., goals against) we can observe a significant reaction of the AARs from the 60-seconds period on for five more periods. The CAARs are significant from the 0-seconds period on. A correction of returns seems to take place in the 120-seconds period, where the AAR is positive.

In PM2, the magnitude of average reaction is considerably larger for goals against (-5.45%) compared to the average reaction to goals (2.75%).

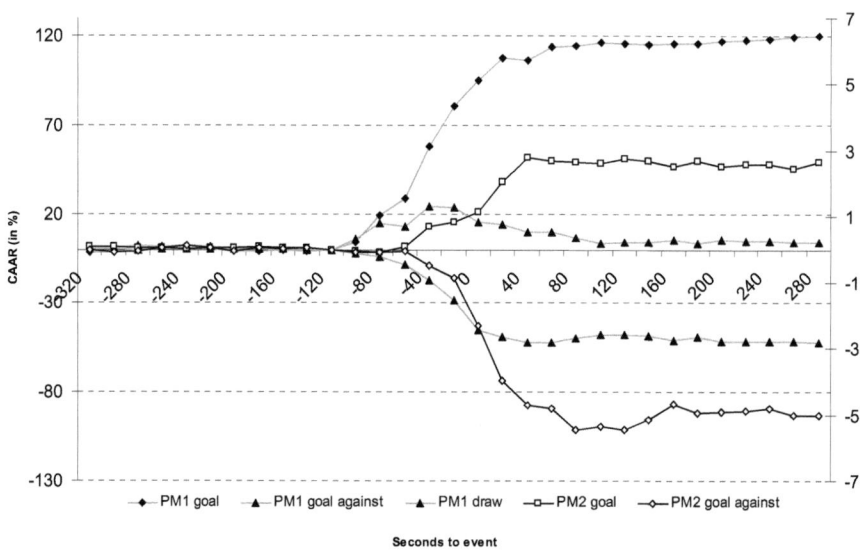

Figure 1: Cumulative Average Abnormal Returns of PM1 (left scale) and PM2 (right scale)

The difference in the magnitude of reaction to goals of each PM is explained by the different horizons of the forecasting goal and the payoff function itself. Thus, since the real-money PM (PM1) traded three stocks that reflected each possible outcome of a single game, the price reaction to events is of higher magnitude than in the play-money market (PM2), where stocks reflect the overall tournament performance of a team. Therefore, the prices of a stock in PM2 potentially include the outcome of several games.

5.2.2 Speed of information incorporation

To compare the speed of information incorporation, we calculate the number of periods with significant AAR (at the 5% level) for each stock and each event i and type r (goal, goal against, [draw]) in the event window, which consists of 12 periods of 20 seconds each:

(5) $\quad$ No. of periods with significant AAR in Event Window$_{i,r} = \sum_{t^* \in T^*} \delta_{i,r,t^*}$,

where

(6) $$\delta_{i,r,t^*} = \begin{cases} 1, \text{ if } |\lambda_t^{AAR}| > tinv(.05) \text{ of event } i \text{ and stock type } r \\ 0, \text{ otherwise}, \end{cases}$$

and $T^* = \{-100,-80,...,120\}$. Therefore, we assume that the information incorporation has ended with the 120-seconds period.

	Avg. no. of periods with significant AAR in Event Window (SD) in PM1		Avg. no. of periods with significant AAR in Event Window (SD) in PM2	
	Periods	Seconds	Periods	Seconds
Goal	3.42 (2.25)	68.4 (45.0)	4.86 (2.26)	97.2 (45.2)
Goal against	3.37 (2.10)	67.4 (42.0)	3.31 (2.27)	66.2 (45.4)
Draw	3.42 (2.30)	68.4 (46.0)	-	-
Total	3.40 (2.20)	**68.0 (44.0)**	4.08 (2.38)	**81.6 (47.6)**

Table 4: Speed of information incorporation

For PM1, the average number of periods with significant AARs is similar for all three types of payoffs, ranging from 3.37 (goal against) to 3.42 (goal and draw) out of 12 periods in the event window (Table 4). However, the standard deviation of slightly more than 2 indicates a rather high variation. On average, PM1 incorporates the new information within 1 minute and 8 seconds (3.4 periods).

In PM2, the range between the types of stocks is greater: 4.86 (sd= 2.26) periods for goals compared to 3.31 periods (sd=2.27) for goals against, indicating a faster reaction to goals against than to goals (Table 4). Accordingly, the average speed of information incorporation here is 1 minute and 22 seconds.

Thus, on average, the time of information incorporation in PM2 is 14 seconds longer than in PM1, which is significant at the 5%-level (two-sided t-test).

5.2.3 Change of predictive accuracy

We use the absolute error (AE) measure to analyze the predictive accuracy of both PMs. We calculate the AE of the stocks corresponding to event i and type r (goal, goal against, (draw)) in the last estimation period t^{before} and in the last event period t^{after}. The error of a stock is the absolute deviation of its price $p_{i,r,t^{before(after)}}$ and its final payoff $d_{i,r}$:

(7) $$AE_{i,r}^{before(after)} = \left| p_{i,r,t^{before(after)}} - d_{i,r} \right|.$$

	Mean AE before event (sd)	Mean AE after event (sd)	Mean relative improvement
PM1			
Goal	4.40 (2.90)	4.19 (2.81)	4.72 % n.s.
Goal against	4.03 (2.61)	2.61 (2.71)	35.02 % ***
Draw	4.22 (2.39)	3.53 (2.55)	13.49 % **
Total	4.21 (2.63)	3.44 (2.75)	**16.24 %** ***
PM2			
Goal	50.73 (45.35)	50.02 (43.76)	1.40 % n.s.
Goal against	45.61 (38.53)	41.43 (39.84)	9.16 % ***
Total	48.17 (41.90)	45.72 (41.76)	**5.09 % ***

Table 5: Change of predictive accuracy
(n.s.: not significant, *: $p < 0.1$, **: $p < 0.05$, ***: $p < 0.01$)

In both PMs, adjustments of prices in reaction to events lead to a higher predictive accuracy, implying an efficient reaction of the markets (Table 5). The magnitude of the total improvement of PM1 (16.24%) is larger than the improvement for PM2 (5.09%), while both improvement rates are significant. This effect, again, can be attributed to the different payoff functions and durations of both PMs. However, the improvement rates for goals against compared to the remaining two (one) type(s) are considerably larger in both PMs. In PM1, the goal stocks' improvement is 4.72% and not significant. In PM2, the improvement of goals against stocks is only 1.40% and again not significant.

Thus, both markets improve their predictive accuracy as a reaction to new events (although not significantly in case of goals, but with the correct sign), while they both assess the negative events in a more accurate way.

5.2.4 Liquidity

While in the real- vs. play-money studies (Rosenbloom and Notz, 2006, Servan-Schreiber et al., 2004), no statements about the markets' properties in terms of liquidity were made, it is especially important to observe liquidity when analyzing continuous price reactions. Although no causal statement can be made about the applicability of event studies with respect to liquidity without a controlled experiment, some descriptive statistics are presented to show the amount of liquidity in PM1 and PM2, where the event studies have shown good results.

The number of traders (454 (sd = 108) in PM1 compared to 906 (sd = 244) in PM2, Table 6) and the number of trades (1,473 (sd = 1,131) in PM1 and 3,625 (sd = 480) in PM2) was significantly lower in PM1. Also, the number of trades per trader and game was significantly lower in PM1 (3.18 (sd = 0.49) trades compared to 3.99 trades (sd = 0.68)). The lower number of trades per trader in PM1 is likely to be attributed to a trading fee of 2% per trade which was charged and which might have prevented participants from trading more frequently.

	PM 1	PM 2	Rel. difference
General liquidity in market			
Total no. of trades during games	45,662	112,364	146.07 % ***
Avg. no. of traders per game (sd)	454 (108)	906 (244)	99.82 % ***
Avg. no. of trades per game (sd)	1,473 (1,131)	3,625 (480)	146.07 % ***
Avg. no. of trades per game per trader (sd)	3.18 (0.49)	3.99 (0.68)	25.74 % ***
Avg. no. of trades per game per stock (sd)	491 (160)	1,812 (566)	269.12 % ***

Table 6: Liquidity in markets
(n.s.: not significant, *: p < 0.1, **: p < 0.05, ***: p < 0.01)

Moreover, with only two stocks which were traded in PM2 per game compared to three in PM1, on average the number of trades in PM1 per stock was 491 compared to 1,812 in PM2.

Thus, considering the indicators of overall and event specific liquidity, it can be inferred that PM1 is less liquid than PM2. Although we cannot draw causal conclusions about the dependence of liquidity on the applicability of event studies in these PMs, the previous analyses indicate that the given liquidity (see Table 6) enabled these markets to perform well.

6. General Discussion

The primary motivation for the application of event studies with data from PMs is the broad range of forecasting applications because they can a) be set up for nearly any future event and b) are less prone to confounding effects due to the flexible forecasting goal.

In this paper, we showed that event study methodology can be applied to PMs with both, play- and real-money investments. Our results show that information is incorporated into stock returns in less than 90 seconds on average in both PMs, however, more slowly in play-money markets. An application of the event study methodology revealed stable and clear reactions to events in both cases, which most likely was also the consequence of the identification and removal of confounding effects. A validation of reactions to events by comparison of the forecast error showed that in both markets, the predictive accuracy increased as consequence of the event reaction, implying an efficient market reaction on average.

Thus, we yield comparably good results for both PMs for the same events regardless of the payoff function and monetary investment scheme, which is an important aspect when setting up PMs or using PMs for event studies. One possible reason why play-money markets performed comparably well as real-money markets was identified by the fact that the play-money PM was considerably more liquid in terms of frequency of trading, number of participants and trading before and after events. With high liquidity, potential uninformed trading in play-money markets (Gruca et al., 2003) can quickly be adjusted by more informed traders. On the other hand, due to the potential absence of uninformed trading, even lower liquidity real-money markets can also perform well. Hence, we conclude that both, play-money PMs with sufficient liquidity and real-money PMs can provide the necessary data for event studies.

However, our study faces some limitations since our data sets differed with respect to stock payoffs and liquidity. Based on these limitations, future research should experimentally test the performance of event study methodology in play-money vs. real-money PM under tightly controlled laboratory conditions where comparable liquidity is ensured. Further, the extension of event study methodology to company internal PMs with low liquidity or a smaller number of participants is a promising area for future research.

References

Berg, J. E. & Rietz, T. A. (2003) Prediction Markets as Decision Support Systems. *Information Systems Frontiers*, 5 (1), 79-93.

Binder, J. L. (1998) The Event Study Methodology Since 1969. *Review of Quantitative Finance and Accounting*, 11 (2), 111–137.

Borghesi, R. (2006) Underreaction to New Information: Evidence from an Online Exchange. *Working Paper. Texas State University.*

Brown, S. J. & Warner, J. B. (1985) Using Daily Stock Returns - The Case of Event Studies. *Journal of Financial Economics*, 14 (1), 3-31.

Chaney, P. K., Devinney, T. M. & Winer, R. (1991) The Impact of New Product Introductions on the Market Value of Firms. *Journal of Business*, 64 (4), 573-610.

Chen, K.-Y. & Plott, C. R. (2002) Information Aggregation Mechanisms: Concept, Design and Implementation for a Sales Forecasting Problem. *Working Paper, California Institute of Technology.*

Chiappori, P.-A., Levitt, S. & Groseclose, T. (2002) Testing Mixed-Strategy Equilibria When Players Are Heterogeneous: The Case of Penalty Kicks in Soccer. *American Economic Review*, 92 (2), 1138-1151.

Christiansen, J. D. (2007) Prediction Markets: Practical Experiments in Small Markets and Behaviours Observed. *Journal of Prediction Markets*, 1 (1), 17-41.

Easton, S. & Uylangco, K. (2007) An Examination of In-Play Sports Betting Using One-Day Cricket Matches. *Journal of Prediction Markets*, 1 (2), 93-109.

Elberse, A. (2007) The Power of Stars: Do Star Actors Drive the Success of Movies? *Journal of Marketing,* 71 (4), 102-120.

Fama, E. F. (1970) Efficient Capital Markets: A Review of Theory and Empirical Work. *Journal of Finance,* 25 (2), 383-417.

Forsythe, R., Rietz, T. A. & Ross, T. W. (1999) Wishes, Expectations and Actions: A Survey on Price Formation in Election Stock Markets. *Journal of Economic Behavior & Organization,* 39 (1), 83-110.

Gruca, T. S., Berg, J. & Cipriano, M. (2003) The Effect of Electronic Markets on Forecasts of New Product Success. *Information Systems Frontiers,* 5 (1), 95-105.

Horsky, D. & Swyngedouw, P. (1987) Does It Pay to Change Your Company's Name? A Stock Market Perspective. *Marketing Science,* 6 (4), 320-335.

Kothari, S. P. & Warner, J. B. (2006) Econometrics of Event Studies. In Eckbo, B. E. (Ed.) *Handbook of Corporate Finance: Empirical Corporate Finance.* Elsevier/North-Holland.

Luckner, S. & Weinhardt, C. (2007) How to Pay Traders in Information Markets? Results from a Field Experiment. *Journal of Prediction Markets,* 1 (2), 1-10.

MacKinlay, C. M. (1997) Event Studies in Economics and Finance. *Journal of Ecomomic Literature,* 35 (3), 13-39.

Manski, C. F. (2006) Interpreting the Predictions of Prediction Markets. *Economic Letters,* 91 (3), 435-429.

McKenzie, A. M., Thomsen, M. R. & Dixon, B. L. (2004) The Performance of Event Study Approaches Using Daily Commodity Futures Returns. *The Journal of Futures Markets,* 24 (6), 533-555.

McWilliams, A. & Siegel, D. (1997) Event Studies in Management Research: Theoretical and Empirical Issues. *The Academy of Management Journal,* 40 (3), 626-657.

Oliven, K. & Rietz, T. A. (2004) Suckers Are Born but Markets Are Made: Individual Rationality, Arbitrage, and Market Efficiency on an Electronic Futures Market. *Management Science,* 50 (3), 336-351.

Ostrover, S. (2005) Employing Information Markets to Achieve Truly Colloborative Sales Forecasting. *Journal of Business Forecasting,* 24 (1), 9-12.

Pennock, D. M., Debnath, S., Glover, E. J. & Giles, C. L. (2002) Modeling Information Incorporation in Markets, with Application to Detecting and Explaining Events. *Pro-*

ceedings of the 18th Conference on Uncertainty in Artificial Intelligence (2002). San Francisco.

Pennock, D. M., Lawrence, S., Giles, L. C. & Nielsen, F. A. (2000) The Power of Play: Efficiency and Forecast Accuracy in Web Market Games. *Working Paper, NEC Research Institute.*

Rosen, R. J. (2006) Merger Momentum and Investor Sentiment: The stock Market Reaction to Merger Announcements. *Journal of Business,* 79 (2), 987–1017.

Rosenbloom, E. S. & Notz, W. (2006) Statistical Tests of Real-Money versus Play-Money Prediction Markets. *Electronic Markets,* 16 (1), 63-69.

Servan-Schreiber, E., Wolfers, J., Pennock, D. M. & Galebach, B. (2004) Prediction Markets: Does Money Matter? *Electronic Markets,* 14 (3), 243-251.

Snowberg, E., Wolfers, J. & Zitzewitz, E. (2007) Partisan Impacts on the Economy: Evidence From Prediction Markets and Close Elections. *Quarterly Journal of Economics,* 122 (2), 807-829.

Spann, M. & Skiera, B. (2003) Internet-Based Virtual Stock Markets for Business Forecasting. *Management Science,* 49 (10), 1310-1326.

Tziralis, G. & Tatsiopoulos, I. (2007) Prediction Markets: An Extended Literature Review. *Journal of Prediction Markets,* 1 (1), 75-91.

Wolfers, J. & Zitzewitz, E. (2004) Prediction Markets. *Journal of Economic Perspectives,* 18 (2), 107-126.

Wolfers, J. & Zitzewitz, E. (2006) Interpreting Prediction Market Prices as Probabilities. *Working Paper, University of Pennsylvania.*

Wolfers, J. & Zitzewitz, E. (2009) Using Markets to Inform Policy: The Case of the Iraq War. *Economica,* 76 (302), 225–250.

Yermack, D. (1997) Good Timing: CEO Stock Option Awards and Company News Announcements. *Journal of Finance,* 52 (2), 449-476.

Appendix: Standard Procedure of Event Studies

When measuring the effect of an event on the stock return, the *abnormal return* (AR) of a stock that was potentially caused by the event has to be determined. Therefore, an expected return of the stock in case the event did not occur is subtracted from the actual return R_{it} of the stock i in time t:

(1) $$AR_{i,t} = R_{i,t} - E(R_{i,t} | X_t).$$

While R_{it} is the actual observable return, different models have been proposed of how to determine the expected return $E(R_{it} | X_t)$, with X_t being the required market data up to period t. The parameters to estimate the expected return are determined in an *estimation window* with the corresponding return model, ranging from $t = T_0 + 1$ to $t = T_1$, with $t = 0$ as the event date. The *event window*, $t = T_1 + 1$ to $t = T_2$, is used to estimate the price of the stock during the occurrence of the event. Due to the event date uncertainty and the possibility that some information might have leaked to the market earlier, the event window usually starts before $t = 0$.

As abnormal returns are observed over a set of stocks (or over several points in time), abnormal returns are aggregated for each period to obtain the joint abnormal return (*cross-sectional aggregation*), leading to *average abnormal returns*:

(2) $$AAR_t = \frac{1}{N} \sum_{i=1}^{N} AR_{i,t}.$$

The expected standard deviation can be calculated using methods as found in Brown and Warner (1985) or MacKinlay (1997).

Subsequently, in order to account for a multiple period event window and to capture all effects, abnormal returns are aggregated, resulting in *cumulated average abnormal returns*:

(3) $$CAAR(t_1,t_2) = \sum_{t=t_1}^{t=t_2} AAR_t .$$

Finally, a two-sided test of the null hypothesis H_0 is applied using a standard statistic (Kothari and Warner, 2006) dividing the (C)AAR by their standard deviation, analyzing whether the returns from the estimation window have significantly changed in the event window both for cumulated or non-cumulated returns:

(4) $$H_0 : E(AAR) = 0 \leftrightarrow H_1 : E(AAR) \neq 0 \text{ and}$$
$$H_0 : E(CAAR) = 0 \leftrightarrow H_1 : E(CAAR) \neq 0 .$$

I want morebooks!

Buy your books fast and straightforward online - at one of the world's fastest growing online book stores! Environmentally sound due to Print-on-Demand technologies.

Buy your books online at
www.get-morebooks.com

Kaufen Sie Ihre Bücher schnell und unkompliziert online – auf einer der am schnellsten wachsenden Buchhandelsplattformen weltweit! Dank Print-On-Demand umwelt- und ressourcenschonend produziert.

Bücher schneller online kaufen
www.morebooks.de

OmniScriptum Marketing DEU GmbH
Heinrich-Böcking-Str. 6-8
D - 66121 Saarbrücken
Telefax: +49 681 93 81 567-9

info@omniscriptum.com
www.omniscriptum.com

Printed by Books on Demand GmbH, Norderstedt / Germany